CAREER SKILLS LIBRARY

Teamwork
Skills

THIRD EDITION

CAREER SKILLS LIBRARY

Communication Skills

Finding A Job

Leadership Skills

Learning the Ropes

Organization Skills

Problem Solving

Professional Ethics and Etiquette

Research and Information Management

Teamwork Skills

FERGUSON

CAREER SKILLS LIBRARY

Teamwork Skills

THIRD EDITION

Ferguson Publishing
An imprint of Infobase Publishing

Teamwork Skills, Third Edition

Ferguson
An imprint of Infobase Publishing
132 West 31st Street
New York NY 10001

Library of Congress Cataloging-in-Publication Data

Teamwork skills. — 3rd ed.
    p. cm. — (Career skills library)
  Includes bibliographical references and index.
  ISBN-13: 978-0-8160-7771-7 (hardcover : alk. paper)
  ISBN-10: 0-8160-7771-1 (hardcover : alk. paper) 1. Teams in the workplace.
[1. Teams in the workplace. 2. Vocational guidance.]
  HD66.M325 2009
  658.4'022—dc22
                                    2009005125

Ferguson books are available at special discounts when purchased in bulk quantities for businesses, associations, institutions, or sales promotions. Please call our Special Sales Department in New York at (212) 967-8800 or (800) 322-8755.

You can find Ferguson on the World Wide Web at http://www.fergpubco.com

Text design by David Strelecky, adapted by Erik Lindstrom
Cover design by Takeshi Takahashi
First edition by Joe Mackall

Printed in the United States of America

MP ML 10 9 8 7 6 5 4 3 2 1

This book is printed on acid-free paper.

CONTENTS

INTRODUCTION

Most of us have been part of a team. Your family acts as a team, dividing the labor and working out relationships. In school, sooner or later you're bound to end up on a group project. You might play sports, participate in the band, sing in a choir, cheer on a pep squad, or serve on a student committee.

You know how teams work . . . and how they don't.

Most corporations and businesses believe in the effectiveness of workplace teams. Millions of dollars are spent each year training employees to work together and get along. Why? Because teams work. They produce greater profits and more satisfied employees.

☛ FACT

Businessman Charles Schwab claimed industrialist Andrew Carnegie paid him a million dollars a year—not for his intelligence or

1

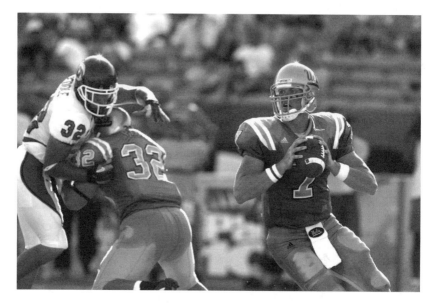

Teamwork is essential in sports and in almost every aspect of life. (Danny Moloshok, AP Photo)

knowledge of steel—but because of Schwab's ability to get along with people.

How are you at getting along with people? Each year thousands of highly skilled people and former A-students fail to fit into corporate teams. Their individual skills are strong, but they can't function as part of a team. And in the modern workforce, only people with strong team skills will be able to make it. Those without these skills will find themselves looking for another job.

Lee Wilkins, manager of human resources for the Gorman-Rupp Company, an international manufacturing firm, puts it this way: "We can teach new hires the job skills they need to succeed. What we can't teach is how to fit in and get along with the rest of the team. And if they can't do that, they'll never make it."

DID YOU KNOW?

Employers surveyed in 2007 by the National Association of Colleges and Employers rated teamwork skills as very-to-extremely important for job candidates.

WHY "DREAM DRAFT PICKS" FAIL TO MAKE CORPORATE DREAM TEAMS

- Can't work as part of a team
- Poor people skills
- Poor communication skills
- Inability to learn and be flexible
- Don't carry their weight
- Lack of dedication to the corporate team
- Negative attitude
- Won't learn from teammates
- Personality conflicts
- Selfishness

If you want to succeed in the workplace, you'll need to know how to work as a member of a team. And if you think it's tough getting along with your algebra classmates, wait till you join the fast-paced, multicultural business world!

And even if you do survive your probation period with the corporate dream team, you're still not off the hook. Now you have to keep your position. Few workers stick with the same job for 20 years anymore. Workers between the ages of 18 and 38 change their jobs—or even their careers—an average of 10 times, according to the U.S. Department of Labor. Jobs and technical skills change as industry changes. We switch jobs or our jobs change. People skills are what keep talented people employed.

All for one and one for all.

—from *The Three Musketeers*

In this book we'll take a close look at corporate teams and the kinds of employees they're seeking. We'll talk about your expectations and theirs, how you can be "people-smart" in today's multicultural world. You'll be surprised how simple it is to become a top draft pick for a business team.

Other topics covered in this book include:

- Developing the proper attitudes and expectations for working in teams

- Learning how interpersonal skills affect you and your team's success

- Having realistic expectations from your workplace and coworkers

- Learning the unwritten rules of your workplace

- Appreciating diversity at work

- Resolving and avoiding team conflicts

- Setting and negotiating goals for your team

THE CORPORATE
DREAM TEAM

When the 2005 Major League Baseball season began, few experts felt that the Chicago White Sox had a chance to make the playoffs, let alone win the World Series. While competitive occasionally over the years, the team had not won a World Series since 1917. The team finished the 2004 season with 83 wins in 162 games—nine games out of first place in their division. The team was built on the long ball and its manager, Ozzie Guillen, had often complained that his players were not competing as a team, but rather selfishly for personal goals and statistics.

Major changes were made to the team during the offseason. The team's general manager decided that the roster needed an overhaul—with a focus on speed, defense, situational hitting, and an overall team-oriented approach. Key players such as Jose Valentin, Carlos Lee, and Magglio Ordonez (responsible for a combined 70 home runs and 206 runs

✔ TRUE OR FALSE?

Are You Ready for the Corporate Dream Team?

1. I don't like interacting with others. But as long as I do my job well, any company would want to hire me.

2. Getting along with others is a key part of being a member of a successful team.

3. It's important to be friends with my coworkers.

Test yourself as you read through this chapter. The answers appear on pages 24–25.

batted in in 2004) were replaced by more team-oriented players such as A. J. Pierzynski, Jermaine Dye, and Scott Podsednik.

Few fans or members of the media believed these acquisitions and the change to a team-oriented philosophy would improve the Sox's record. In fact, many national baseball experts picked the Sox to finish fourth or even fifth in their division.

The experts' gloomy predictions seemed right on target when the 2005 season began. The White Sox opened the season slowly—splitting their first six games. Then the lessons on team play that manager Ozzie Guillen had stressed in spring training kicked in. The White Sox began to maximize their assets and play winning team baseball. They

Teamwork played an integral role in the Chicago White Sox's World Championship season in 2005. (John G. Mabanglo/epa/Corbis)

executed the hit and run, advanced and scored runners with sacrifice bunts and flies, and pitched and hit in the clutch. They also didn't point fingers at teammates who weren't playing up to their abilities. They pulled together, realizing that each player brought a different skill to the team. The new players such as speedster Scott Podsednik, steady Jermaine Dye, and the fiery but talented A. J. Pierzynski were immediately accepted and counted on to help win games. In short, the White Sox did anything they could to win. This style of play even earned a nickname—"Grinderball."

After their mediocre start, the White Sox won 10 of their next 15 games. At the end of the season, the Sox were in first place and headed to the playoffs!

The White Sox only got better in postseason play. They beat the Boston Red Sox, the 2004 World Series winners, and the Anaheim Angels to advance to the World Series. Then they swept the Houston Astros in four games to win the World Series and complete a 11-win, one-loss playoff run. Jermaine Dye was named the World Series Most Valuable Player.

Viewed as individual players, the White Sox probably didn't strike much fear in the minds of their opponents. But these individuals came together to create something magical: a greatness no player could have achieved on his own. These men became a World Championship team.

We [the 2005 Chicago White Sox] are the Cinderella of the playoffs. It's a great feeling when they don't pick you and all of a sudden you make it. But don't change a thing—just play White Sox baseball. You don't win [99] games just because.

**—Chicago White Sox Manager Ozzie Guillen
on MLB.com, 10/02/2005**

WHY TEAMS?

When a poor boy named Sam came up with an idea for full-scale discount operations in small towns, few people listened. Sam had a vision for an organization in which employees considered themselves a family, part of the team.

Sam worked in other people's stores until he could beg and borrow enough money to open his own. He encouraged suggestions from his employees and put their ideas to good use. His business grew, and Sam opened other stores. He visited each "team" regularly. Several mornings a week Sam could be found sitting on a crate or standing in front of a crowd of employees and leading the company cheer: "Give me a W! Give me an A! Give me an L! Give me an M! Give me an A! Give me an R! Give me a T!"

We're all working together; that's the secret.

—Sam Walton

When Sam Walton died in 1992, he left a fortune of $2.5 billion and 1,720 Wal-Mart stores spread across the United States. His philosophy lives on today. In 2003 and 2004, *Fortune* magazine named Wal-Mart as the most admired company in America. The company employs more than 2 million associates worldwide at more than 7,200 stores. Most biographers credit Walton's success in large measure to his unique ability to make his employees feel like a family and operate like a team.

Small teams are becoming the basic unit of corporate organization. Why are major corporations using teams to get the job done? Because teams work.

WHY ARE CORPORATE TEAMS GROWING IN POPULARITY?

- Technological innovations have created tasks, duties, and projects that are too complicated for an individual to handle alone.

- Corporate downsizing has thinned the ranks of middle managers and required more responsibility and teamwork from lower-level employees.

- As corporations become increasingly larger and multinational, they no longer focus on one type of product or service. This creates a need for more teams to solve problems, oversee workflow, and facilitate communication and production between work units.

WHY ME?

You land your dream job. You feel you've arrived. Confident it was your unsurpassed skills that brought you such success, you report for work. It's your first day at your new job, and you're ready to take on the world single-handedly.

You are assigned to work as a member of a team on a number of customer service-related projects, but you barely listen as your manager stresses team-work and breaks down everyone's job duties. You don't even really listen to anyone else's ideas in the meetings, even if they might be useful. You give everyone lip-service, but you can't wait to get back to your cubicle to brainstorm ways that you can improve the company.

For 90 days you come up with ideas to increase your company's interaction with its customers. Each week you make sure your brilliance shines. Your reports have to be better than anyone else's.

After three months, you're ready for your first evaluation. Confident of your personal success, you march into your boss's office.

"Sorry," your boss begins. "It doesn't appear to be working out for you as we'd hoped. You're just not cut out for our team here. I'm afraid we're going to have to let you go."

You've been cut from the corporate dream team.

The scene happens over and over, usually within the first 90 days of a new career. The battle isn't over once you've landed your dream job. You have to prove yourself. You have to earn your place on your team by fitting in.

One executive, who has managed over a dozen businesses on the East Coast, put it this way: "The

The battle isn't over once you've landed your dream job. You have to prove yourself.

ability to get along with people doesn't just come in handy. You won't survive without it. Somebody said it was a jungle out there? Ha! Compared to what's really waiting out there in the world of high finance, jungles are for wimps."

It will be up to you to prove you can work as part of a team.

TEAMWORK! TEAMWORK! TEAMWORK!

Teamwork is the process whereby a group of people pool their resources and skills to work together and achieve a common goal. In other words, your boss will be looking for two things from his dream team: team and work.

Putting the "Team" in Teamwork

Your mother told you first. Try to get along with people. Make friends. Play nicely. Share.

Now you're in the big leagues. You can't just pick up your bat and go home anymore. Stakes are high, often in the millions of dollars. One Chicago stock-broker, fully aware of the high stakes in the business world, said: "This company could lose more money in 60 seconds than I could make in 60 years. Nothing I do ends with me. We're in this together."

No matter how skilled or talented you may be, if you can't get along with other members of your team, you won't last long.

Teamwork is the process whereby a group of people pool their resources and skills to work together and achieve a common goal.

TEAMS=Together Each Accomplishes More Success!

—from James Lundy's *Teams: How to Develop Peak Performance Teams for World-Class Results*

Experts advise that teamwork can improve productivity 10 to 40 percent.

Recognizing the Importance of Teams

Kala learned about teams the hard way. She received three job offers before she finished her senior year at Oklahoma University. After many interviews and sleepless nights, she decided on an entry-level position at Estée Lauder. She liked the hours and the promise of rapid advancement to management levels.

She was assigned to sell perfume in a posh department store. Kala was disappointed with her coworkers. For one thing, they were older than her recruiter had led her to expect. Kala missed her college friends. These women hadn't even attended college.

But no matter. Kala saw her job on the department store floor as a jumping-off point. She'd show them what she could do and move up fast.

Life didn't work out that way. Kala's team seemed to read her thoughts. They didn't like being used as a "step" on someone else's career ladder. On every break, Kala left the department instead of trying to get to know her coworkers. Her team resented Kala's inattention to detail and her standoffishness. They sensed her lack of interest in any part of the business that didn't directly affect her.

READ MORE ABOUT IT

Maxwell. John C. *The 17 Essential Qualities of a Team Player: Becoming the Kind of Person Every Team Wants.* Nashville, Tenn.: Thomas Nelson, 2002.

Maxwell. John C. *The 17 Indisputable Laws of Teamwork Workbook: Embrace Them and Empower Your Team.* Nashville, Tenn.: Thomas Nelson, 2003.

Parker, Glenn M. *Team Players and Teamwork: New Strategies for Developing Successful Collaboration.* 2d ed. San Francisco: Jossey-Bass, 2008.

Peragine, John N. *365 Low or No Cost Workplace Teambuilding Activities: Games and Exercises Designed to Build Trust & Encourage Teamwork Among Employees.* Ocala, Fla.: Atlantic Publishing Company, 2008.

Stowell, Steven J., and Stephanie S. Mead. *The Team Approach: With Teamwork Anything Is Possible.* Sandy, Utah: CMOE Press, 2007.

A year later, Kala reflects on her first weeks at Estee Lauder. "I couldn't believe the people I worked with didn't like me. In college, I could get along with anybody. So I figured it must be their fault. They resented me because I was making more sales than they were. I just wanted to do my job and move on."

But when Kala's three-month trial period ended, she was in for a shock. "I was expecting praise and rewards for all the sales I made. But the whole evaluation sounded lukewarm. And the biggest notation said: 'Not a team player!' I couldn't believe it. I don't know if I was more surprised that someone would say I wasn't a team player, or more shocked that management would put so much emphasis on teamwork. I left the company before they could fire me."

SURF THE WEB: WORKING IN TEAMS

13 Ways to Encourage Teamwork
http://www.askmen.com/money/
successful_100/115_success.html

Manual for Working in Teams
http://www.analytictech.com/mb021/
teamhint.htm

Surviving the Group Project: A Note on Working in Teams
http://web.cba.neu.edu/~ewertheim/
teams/ovrvw2.htm#Introduction

Team Building
http://www.meetingwizard.org/
meetings/team-building.cfm

Companies do care about teams. Experts advise that teamwork can improve productivity 10–40 percent. Teams in the workplace are expected to be more than the sum of individual members. That means team members may have to spend as much energy working at team relationships as they will getting the job done.

Workers need interpersonal team skills that will enable them to fit in. Jerry Richmond managed chain stores for Sears and Woolworth before owning his own retail business. He says, "I've seen talented people come and go. But my advice for students is: The best skill you can develop is to get along with people. Cooperation with your team covers a multitude of sins."

Don't Forget the "Work" in Teamwork

Developing good team skills will help prepare you for working with a group of people. You should come to think of your coworkers as a team, whether or not your company officially designates team units.

But forming a team is only part of the picture. You can't forget the second half of teamwork: work. If you forget the work in teamwork, you may end up with some nice friends . . . who can go job hunting with you. Companies expect teams to produce.

A saying that goes around Goldman Sachs, an investment bank, is, "Corporations pay for performance, not for potential."

Interpersonal skills are essential for teamwork. But teamwork is more than getting along with others.

Your new employer will expect your team to work. You'll have to get the job done. Together, you will need to tackle problems, complete tasks, meet milestones—work.

Teamwork is so important in medical coding. The coder is a key member of the physician's or facility team. It takes a team to keep the practice/facility solvent and get paid for services rendered. The physicians must work with the coders and vice versa to stay up to date on changing regulations, coding rules, etc. in order to continue to report services correctly.

—Deborah Grider, president of the National Advisory Board of the American Academy of Professional Coders and owner of Deborah Grider & Associates LLC, a health care consulting firm

LEARNING FROM EXPERIENCE

When Larry joined a California team of researchers, he took with him a school experience in teamwork. In junior high, Larry and four friends formed an extracurricular group to compete in Odyssey of the Mind, a science competition. Their task was spelled out for them. Each team had to demonstrate a scientific principle through a physical representation.

In certain ways, Larry and his friends made a great team. They got along well, joked, and encouraged each other. Larry wasn't sold on his buddy's idea to build a papier-mâché volcano. He knew it lacked originality. But Larry didn't want to hurt his friend's feelings, so he went along with it.

Larry looked forward to the team's meetings. Everybody had a great time, although not much work was accomplished. But between the horseplay and refreshments, the team managed to throw together a volcano that erupted on command.

In the end, however, Larry's team bombed. They placed next to last in the competition. They thought they knew what it meant to be a good team. But Larry admits his group of friends had no idea what teamwork required.

Larry took his school team experience with him to his first job. For the last year, Larry has been part of a research-development team. He's discovered that good relationships are necessary. But that's not all there is to it.

Referring to his research team, Larry explains: "At first, before we knew each other, it seemed like we got more work done. We each did our own thing and kept out of each other's way. Then when we got to know and like each other, it was harder to get anything done. We had a great time together. But we weren't getting anywhere. It reminded me of my old Odyssey of the Mind group."

But Larry had learned from his mistakes. With his Odyssey of the Mind buddies, he hadn't wanted to risk damaging friendships just to get the job done.

This time, he wanted friends, but he knew they had to get the job done.

Larry talked to his team about the problem. Finally, they began to focus on their goals. Team members made compromises and the team started to find its way. They plowed through and discovered they could accomplish their goals if they made themselves and each other accountable for the work.

"And that," Larry says, "is when we started working together as a team."

Later, in Larry's first-year evaluation with his supervisor, he discovered how vital teamwork was to his employers. The work his team accomplished together weighed more heavily in the evaluation than anything Larry had done on his own.

TEAMWORK BAGGAGE

As you leave school and head for your new job, take some time to assess the teamwork skills you practiced while you were a student. There are certain

TEAMWORK SKILLS TO . . .

Take Along	Leave Behind
Personal responsibility	Personal glory
Ability to motivate the team	"Star" mentality
Constructive competitive spirit	Destructive competitive spirit
Ability to look like your team	Old school uniform
Ability to laugh at yourself	Locker-room jokes
Ability to please your new boss	Your old coach's ways of doing things

skills you'll want to take with you and others you'll need to leave behind.

☛ FACT

Even animals are into teamwork. When geese fly in the "V" formation, they can travel 70 percent faster than when they fly alone.

Teams work, and employers believe in them. That's why businesses look for people with good team skills.

✍ EXERCISE

- Make up your own definition of teamwork.

- List all the teams you've been a part of. Which of these teams worked best? Why do you think that team succeeded?

- Pretend that you are assembling a team to complete a project. How would you organize the group? What skills would you want your teammates to have? Not have?

You may think you've got it made once you pass that interview and get that job offer. But you haven't. You're on probation. And it's not merely a case of what your boss thinks about you. Your people skills have to work on your entire work team.

If you want a spot on the corporate dream team, you may have to change your ideas about what makes a dream player. Paul Kaponya, a management consultant for several leading corporations, says: "Experience and validated studies indicate that the single most important factor affecting success and failure is the ability to work effectively with others."

Want to make it in the majors? Teamwork is the key.

✔ TRUE OR FALSE: ANSWERS

Are You Ready for the Corporate Dream Team?

1. I don't like interacting with others. But as long as I do my job well, any company would want to hire me.

False. You need to be a team player to survive in today's workplace. Downsizing and globalization have created demand for strong team-oriented workers who can put their needs/ambitions aside for the better of the team and company.

2. Getting along with others is a key part of being a member of a successful team.

True. Successful teams feature workers with a wide variety of personalities and backgrounds who have put aside their differences for the common good.

3. It's important to be friends with my coworkers.

False. You, of course, want to get along with your coworkers, but you don't have to be friends. Some of the best teams are those that feature civil and productive—but not overly friendly—relationships between their members.

Too-friendly teams often result in a lot of fun, but too-little work being accomplished.

IN SUMMARY . . .

- Small teams are becoming the basic unit of corporate organization due to technological innovations, corporate downsizing, and the growth of global companies.

- Teamwork skills are among the most sought-after qualities in job candidates.

- Remember: *Team* and *Work.* It is not enough just to be a good team worker; you need to produce results with the members of your team.

- Friendships among team members are a good thing, but they should not interfere with the work the team must accomplish.

- Bring the following teamwork skills with you when you transition from school to work: personal responsibility, the ability to motivate others, constructive competitiveness, the ability to look like your team, a sense of humor about yourself, and the ability to please your new boss.

2

BECOME
PEOPLE SMART

*Here lies one who knew how to get around him men
who were cleverer than himself.*

—Industrialist Andrew Carnegie's
self-written epithet

Christine and Beth beat out a tough crowd of
applicants to join an established, Texas-based
investment firm. Beth had stronger computer skills
than Christine and also brought along a little experience in sales. Although their educational backgrounds were similar, Beth made better grades in
college.

But a year later, Christine found herself on the
fast track to success. Beth still had her job, but she
was looking for a new one. She knew she'd never get
anywhere in the firm, and her supervisor agreed.

✔ TRUE OR FALSE?

Are You People Smart?

1. Knowing your coworkers' strengths and weaknesses is an important tool for building good teamwork skills.

2. Politics and religion are acceptable topics of conversation in the workplace.

3. You should never compromise with other members of a team. It will make you look weak.

Test yourself as you read through this chapter. The answers appear on pages 39–41.

What happened? Why did Christine succeed her first year on the job, but Beth—with her stronger skills—didn't?

One of the members on Christine's and Beth's team confided, "I knew from that first week which one would make it. Christine was people smart. Beth wasn't. It's as simple as that."

Business guru Gordon Wainwright says, "Your success in your organization will depend in large measure on how well you deal with the other people in it."

Discover all you can about your coworkers so you can build strong working relationships.

PLAYING DETECTIVE

Now that you know how vital being a team member is—now that you're convinced that if the team doesn't buy into you, you're out—what can you do about it?

Become a detective. Discover all you can about your coworkers so you can build strong working relationships. Can you read between the lines as people talk? Can you decipher body language when they're silent? Do you have a feeling for who likes to be left alone and who's offended when you don't include him?

Imagine it's your first day at your new job. Your team (Rachel, Missy, Bruno, and Slick) heads for lunch. You tag along and observe.

The five of you take your seats around the linen-covered table, Rachel taking the unofficial head. Poor Missy loses her balance as Slick brushes her aside and takes a seat next to Rachel. Missy walks silently, eyes down, and sits stiffly next to Slick. You take the chair across from Missy as Bruno plops between you and Rachel.

"I'm sick of this place," Bruno says. He picks up the menu, glances at it, and snaps it shut. Sighing deeply, he leans back, one arm over the back of his chair.

Missy hasn't looked up from her menu.

"What are you having, Rachel?" Slick asks, sipping his water. It doesn't appear that he's reading his own menu.

Rachel carefully closes her menu and greets some coworkers she notices at the adjacent table. She speaks to you, rather than answering Slick directly.

"The fish is quite good here. So's the salad and the chicken marsala."

Bruno grunts. His eyes roll toward the ceiling.

The waiter arrives and starts with Missy. "And what would you like?" he says.

None of us is as smart as all of us.

—Japanese proverb

Missy's eyes peek over the top of the menu. "Umm, I'll take the . . ." She straightens her back even more and tugs on the collar of her suit jacket. "Would you please come back to me?" she asks softly.

"Roughy, orange roughy" Slick says, his teeth shining like a shark's. "And salad."

Rachel orders. "I'll have the chicken marsala, crisp salad with light dressing on the side, iced tea, no sugar, baked potato with light sour cream on the side and no butter. Thank you."

Bruno orders spaghetti and warns the waiter not to overcook it this time and to bring him extra garlic bread. He shakes his head at your order.

Missy swallows hard. "I guess I'll have the same," she says, motioning to you, but not looking at you.

Then you wait for your food. And you keep on observing.

Play detective. If you had been paying attention, you would have learned a number of things about your coworkers. For example, Rachel is at least the unofficial leader, commanding deference from the others. She is probably orderly, organized, and possibly someone to keep your eye on as a mentor. She knows how to network (greeting coworkers at the adjacent table), and she knows what she wants. It would probably be worth your time to understand what she expects from you on the job. To earn her respect, you'll have to be organized and efficient.

Slick may be someone you'll have to look out for. Watch him to see if he's willing to do anything to look good to the higher-ups. Unfortunately, there are a lot of "Slicks" out there. If you're a good detective, you'll know when to watch your back.

Bruno is the kind of guy who will likely criticize everything you do. You can learn to get along with him, but don't expect him to encourage you on the job. Be careful not to get caught up in his negativism. You may not want to be labeled as belonging to Bruno's camp.

Obviously Missy appears shy and weak. But don't write her off. Never write off anybody on your team. Think of ways you can encourage quiet members. Ask her questions in her area of expertise. Ask for her opinion. You may be surprised at what she has to offer. And you may be the one who can help her realize her potential and become more effective on the team.

The more you know about the members of the team, the better chance you'll have for a smooth transition and good team relationships.

The more you know about the members of the team, the better chance you'll have for a smooth transition and good team relationships. You don't need to box everybody into categories your first week, but an idea of each member's personality type, learning style, and role can help you understand the dynamics of your team.

ACCEPTING TEAM MEMBERS

Although you may think that your way is the right way, you're not on your team to change your teammates. You're there to learn how best to work with them and achieve team goals.

So what do you do when you meet a "Bruno"? You accept him. Instead of trying to change his behavior, adapt your own. Anticipate his behavior based on how you've seen him act in other situations. Don't let him take you by surprise. Be prepared. When you ask for his input, don't expect a compliment. Brace yourself for criticism. Pick out any parts of his critique that will help your performance, and let the rest roll off you. You know his nature. That's okay. He may have said something you can use.

People can sense when someone accepts them, faults and all. And they generally respond to that person. Your job is not to judge the people on your team, but to help them—and to let them help you—reach team goals.

The ability to deal with people is as purchasable a commodity as sugar or coffee. And I pay more for that ability than for any other under the sun.

—John D. Rockefeller, industrialist

ADAPTING YOUR BEHAVIOR

Once you've accepted your team, adapt your behavior to the needs of the individual. Learn what it takes to make each person on your team comfortable with you. If Missy seems more comfortable talking to you in a straight-backed, feet-on-the-floor position, follow her lead and sit up straight. If Bruno is more laid back, you can do that. Learn to adapt to your team, even in the little things. Rachel loves lists and memos. Give them to her. And go ahead—tell Slick his haircut looks great.

Getting to know the people you work with isn't the same as knowing about them. You may never know the names of their pets, but you should understand their strengths and weaknesses.

PUTTING IT ALL TOGETHER

Every day you have countless chances to use and develop your interpersonal skills. A one-on-one relationship with a friend can be hard enough. No matter how well you get along, you'll run into problems. You want to ice skate, and he wants to swim.

On a working team, you'll need your people skills more than ever. Not only do you have to get along with these people, you have to work together and produce. With so many different personalities and opinions, making even the smallest decisions can be hard. You need to learn how best to handle members of your team.

On a working team, you'll need your people skills more than ever.

Here's an example of a petty but typical workplace problem that can disrupt teamwork. You have been on the job for only three weeks. Management is recarpeting your offices, but it's up to you and two coworkers to decide on the color. Quiet Tim, the person you get along with best in the office, asks you to side with him and choose red. Aggressive Annie, who's obviously on the fast track to success in the corporation, is demanding green. What do you do?

As with most relationships, there is no easy answer. If you have a strong preference and it matters to you, you probably should express your opinion.

But if you're people smart, there are several things you'll do to handle each team member. For instance, don't deal behind Annie's back. If she's as sharp as you think she is, she'll know. And she won't forget. She's not someone you want to antagonize. If she's on the fast track, she's doing something right. You can learn from her. Ask her why she thinks green is the way to go. Listen (don't forget eye contact) while she answers you. If you end up choosing red anyway, do it honestly. Tell her you understand her viewpoint, but tell her you're going to have to go red this time.

If your vote is green, be ready to explain why. If you're quiet, like Tim, explaining your decision might not be easy. But both parties need to understand your rationale. Ask Tim to explain his preference. He may need encouragement to say openly what he said privately. You may want to explain your choice to him privately and make sure he understands.

You might suggest the three of you agree on a blue carpet. Behind the best negotiations are people who are people smart. (Chapter 6 deals with negotiations and compromises.)

Arguing the color of a carpet may sound stupid, but offices have gone to war over less.

THE PROFESSIONAL TEAM

Part of being people smart is understanding the nature of a professional relationship. Your coworkers are not your buddies—not at work anyway. You are professionals working together to accomplish a goal.

Nancy had worked at a city newspaper for six months, long enough to be horrified at Cam's (the newest employee) unprofessional mistake. "She and I were walking past the office of our features editor, who was in deep discussion with her assistant. They were debating whether they should run a story on the Summer FoodFest or the new Jackson Pollock exhibit at the art museum in the upcoming issue. Before I knew what happened, Cam leaned into the editor's office and said, 'I'd go with the FoodFest. More people are interested in food than art.' The whole office fell silent. We're pretty informal. But you just don't interject your opinions into a private discussion between two top editors."

Your coworkers are not your buddies—not at work anyway. You are professionals working together to accomplish a goal.

Work relationships are very different from personal relationships. Although you may get along very well with your manager, it is important to remember that he or she is your boss, not a casual friend, and deserves your utmost respect. (Kim Eriksen/zefa/Corbis)

If you want to make it as part of a professional team, dress, speak, and act professionally.

TEAM PRIVACY

Hopefully you will become part of a team that works. Your interpersonal skills will help you win friends and strengthen your team. But no matter how comfortable you feel with your teammates, you're not home. Be careful what you bring with you from home. Work is not the place to spill your guts.

Laurie felt nervous her first week teaching at a private school. She also had a tendency to talk too much when she was nervous.

On her second day of school, Laurie ate lunch with one of the friendliest teachers. When the woman commented on Laurie's rings, Laurie started in on family stories. "This one is an heirloom my father gave me. My mother bought me this one when I was in college. And," Laurie continued, going for the funny bone, "this is the one my husband bought me our first year out of graduate school—the year he was rich and famous."

Good teams aren't possible if you can't get along with team members.

WHAT NOT TO TALK ABOUT AT WORK

- Financial matters
- Politics
- Relationships/sex
- Religion
- Weights/diets
- Illness/death
- Controversial issues in the news

SAFE TOPICS TO DISCUSS AT WORK

- Books
- Sports
- Current (noncontroversial) events
- Weather
- Entertainment
- Movies
- Vacations/Travel
- Family
- Work
- Hobbies

Laurie sensed immediately that her coworker's attitude toward her changed. But she didn't realize the impact of that heart-to-heart until her first teacher evaluation. The incident had been discussed among the teachers and made its way back to the principal: "Laurie brags at lunch about all her jewelry and her rich family."

Matters of personal finance are probably best kept private. An executive in a Chicago firm said he loses confidence in workers who worry about their own finances. "I always figure they'll go to the highest bidder. I can't count on their loyalty."

You may well end up taking your services to the highest bidder. That's your privilege. But it's not people smart to advertise it.

There are formalities between the closest of friends.

—Japanese proverb

STUDY TO GET SMART

Good teams aren't possible if you can't get along with team members. Learn to study people. Your efforts will pay off. Strong interpersonal skills may keep your company from getting rid of you when they downsize. Working teams are highly esteemed because they bring profits. It's great to be goal oriented in the business world. But you'll never reach those goals unless you become people smart.

✔ TRUE OR FALSE: ANSWERS

Are You People Smart?

1. Knowing your coworkers' strengths and weaknesses is an important tool for building good teamwork skills.

True. Understanding your coworkers' strengths and weaknesses will help you work better with

✍ EXERCISE

- Run a test for yourself. Experiment on a particular group or class. Don't tell them what you're doing, but begin applying your people-smart skills. Figure out how to encourage each person in your class. See if you can make a difference in your individual relationships. After one week, analyze how your new attitude has affected the group or class or an individual.

- For one day, write your own "Translation Book" of body language. See how many gestures and signals you can detect.

- Organize a school-related activity (such as a dance, awards dinner, or fundraiser) using your people-smart skills. Study your classmates' personality types to determine who would best handle various aspects of the project. Once the event is complete, assess your people-smart skills to learn what you did right and wrong

members of your team. Your job is not to change your coworkers, but work with them to meet team goals.

2. Politics and religion are acceptable topics of conversation in the workplace.

False. Discussing hot-button issues such as politics, religion, sex, etc. is a quick path to team dissension. Save these potentially contentious topics for time with your friends or family.

3. You should never compromise with other members of a team. It will make you look weak.

False. Compromise is part of successful team building. It is okay to occasionally disagree with team members, but do it constructively and not every time you have a difference of opinion. Pick your battles when disagreeing with team members. Save your objections for key issues affecting a project, not every minor point of contention.

IN SUMMARY . . .

- Knowing your teammates' strengths, weaknesses, moods, and personalities will help you interact better with your group, anticipate potential problems and disagreements, and develop your own interpersonal skills.

- Use and develop your interpersonal skills daily.

- If you want to be treated as a professional, dress, speak, and act professionally.

- Save your private business for home. Exercise discretion in your conversations with coworkers.

3

UNDERSTANDING TEAM CULTURE

On Mike's first day of work, he arrived downtown so early he had to park his car in darkness. As he opened the glass door to the 40-story office high rise, his heart wouldn't stop pounding. He straightened his tie while he waited for the elevator. As he stepped off onto his floor, Mike thought, "This is it. All my dreams have been fulfilled."

Ten hours later Mike crowded with his coworkers into the stuffy elevator, loosened his tie, and thought, "That was the worst day of my life. I'll never make it." Mike's dream had turned into a nightmare.

Mike had expected the glitzy job his recruiter described. Etched in his mind were scenes from movies, a meteoric rise to wealth and fame, starring Mike. However, the realities of his job were far from glamorous. He had a lot of tough work ahead of him, some of which was rather tedious, but nevertheless important and demanding. Mike could tell

Do You Understand Team Culture?

1. It's important to learn what your employer expects of you on the job.

2. I can wear whatever I want to work.

3. Learning how to read body language is a key tool for interacting successfully with your team.

Test yourself as you read through this chapter. The answers appear on pages 62–63.

it would be a while before he would advance in the company.

One of the first tasks you'll have when managing your new career is to adjust your expectations.

GET REAL

A successful job transition involves a shift from thinking about yourself to thinking about your team.

The following questions were put to people in a variety of careers after they were newly hired, then a year or two after they had been on the job: (1) What were your top expectations when you joined your work team? What were your chief concerns? (2) At the end of the year, what were your expectations? What were your chief concerns?

A successful job transition involves a shift from thinking about yourself to thinking about your team. Expect success for your team. Developing pride in the way your team works together and achieves goals is a good way to ensure success.

THE REAL WORLD

As you step off that elevator and into your first job, you're not the only one with expectations. Your employers have expectations too.

Interviews with over 20 personnel and team managers turned up the following expectations:

- Get to work on time (or early).

- Put in more hours than required.

- Learn from coworkers.

- Be curious—ask questions of everyone on the team.

- Master necessary skills.

- Meet (or beat) deadlines.

- Cooperate unselfishly with the team.

- Dress and act professionally.

- Contribute to the fulfillment of team goals.

- Be responsible and dependable—someone the team can count on.

A BRAVE NEW WORLD

Beginning a new job is a lot like moving to a foreign country. Don't be fooled if the people there look

TOP EXPECTATIONS

New Workers	Workers After the First Year
Praise for getting to work on time	An understanding that being on time is expected
Praise for working late or on weekends to finish projects	Appreciation by my boss that I may occasionally work extra to finish projects, but a realization that this is the requirement of many jobs
Constant affirmation that I am doing a good job	Occasional positive support from managers during projects and in performance reviews
A promotion by the end of the year	Steady movement up the career ladder at the company
A raise after six months	Steady raises based on job performance and duties
Coworkers who are my best friends	Strong relationships with coworkers built on respect; may include friendships
A friendly relationship with my boss	A strong relationship with my boss based on job performance and communication; may include friendship
Rave reviews on my first evaluation	Positive reviews on future evaluations
Recognition for my contribution	Recognition for personal contributions, but also for my ability to work as a member of a team
Understanding when I was late for a good reason	Understanding that I may occasionally be late for a very good reason (medical emergency, etc.), but the knowledge that I let my boss and coworkers down with a high number of late arrivals
Somebody to tell me what to do and how to do it	A boss who tells me how to do things and gives me feedback about my work, but who also trusts me to work independently or with little oversight on tasks and projects

somewhat like you and your office computer is just like yours at home. It's a whole new world, with different customs and a culture you are going to have to figure out.

Figuring out a team's culture and customs isn't always easy. If you don't appreciate the fact that you're in a foreign land and have a lot to learn, you'll make your job that much harder. Missionaries and businesspeople who move to other countries often report that culture shock lasts longer in countries that are most like the United States. Why? Because an American may feel at home in London. The language and clothes are nearly identical to what he or she is used to. But the false sense of familiarity breeds discontent. The expatriate is not home. If the worker doesn't acknowledge the differences soon, he or she may never adjust.

The same is true in the business world. Learn to discern the culture and customs of your team.

Teamwork is essential in real estate development. You must have architects, designers, and contractors who can bring their individual ideas and experience to a project to help create a strong team. And when you have a strong team working to accomplish the same goal, the results will be amazing.

—Julie Norris, vice president, McHugh Development & Construction Inc.

LAWS OF THE LAND

You may be able to get your first ideas of team culture and customs before you show up for work. Read all you can about your company, including mission statements, annual reports, press kits, or any other literature your employer may give you. Go to the library and check out articles about your company. Visit the company's website to read about its history, departments, staff, and the products it produces or the services it offers. And most important, be observant of the unwritten rules of your company by observing how people dress, speak, and conduct themselves and business in general.

How to Dress on the Job

It may not be stated in your company policy manual, but if everyone in your office is wearing a suit and tie, don't come to work in sweats. Take your cue from people who have worked there a long time. Be conservative when you start out. Don't let the way you dress detract from who you are and what you have to offer. Don't be the most dressy or least dressy in your department. Even if your company seems fairly creative and laid back, start out conservative or mainstream, studying the clothing and looks of your coworkers; then adjust your look accordingly.

You might not think dressing well at work makes a difference, but it does. Ninety-three percent of

Don't let the way you dress detract from who you are and what you have to offer.

READ MORE ABOUT IT

Henderson, Veronique, and Pat Henshaw. *Image Matters for Men: How to Dress for Success!* London, U.K.: Hamlyn, 2007.

Lenius, Oscar. *A Well-Dressed Gentleman's Pocket Guide.* London, U.K.: Prion, 2006.

Lerner, Dick. *Dress Like the Big Fish: How to Achieve the Image You Want and the Success You Deserve.* Omaha, Neb.: Bel Air Fashions Press, 2008.

Peres, Daniel. *Details Men's Style Manual: The Ultimate Guide for Making Your Clothes Work for You.* New York: Gotham, 2007.

Weingarten, Rachel C. *Career and Corporate Cool.* Hoboken, N.J.: Wiley, 2007.

executives surveyed in 2007 by OfficeTeam said that an employee's style of dress influences his or her chances of promotion. One-third of respondents said that job attire "significantly" affects an employee's chance of advancement.

Level of Familiarity

When it comes to friendships with your teammates, follow their lead. Be friendly and professional to

It is important to take your style cues from other workers at your company. If most of your coworkers wear business suits and other dressier outfits, then it is a good idea to do so yourself. (KMSS/zefa/Corbis)

everyone, but don't force a friendship out of desperation or loneliness. Don't assume you'll be included right away. Let them invite you.

Some people don't kid around—ever. Don't be the loudest person at the lunch table. And save the locker-room jokes for another audience.

Don't assume that because your boss is friendly, you're his or her friend. Don't go to a first-name basis unless you're clearly told to do so.

Lee Wilkins, manager of human resources at Gorman-Rupp Company, laments the unprofessional behavior of many first-year employees. "Last month one of our interns, on her way out, hollered across the room, 'Hey, Lee! Wanna come with?' I said

DOS AND DON'TS
OF DRESSING FOR WORK

Do wear

- Simple, tailored clothing that presents a professional appearance (even if you have an entry-level job)

- Basic, neutral colors (such as gray, tan, black, brown, and navy) that allow you to mix and match outfits easily

- Clothing that fits and allows you to present yourself in the most tasteful and professional manner

- Quality shoes and other accessories, such as belts

- A hairstyle that is fashionable, professionally styled, and clean

Don't wear

- Sweats

- T-shirts with advertising slogans or potentially offensive graphics

- Too baggy or tight clothing

- Shorts

- Athletic shoes or sandals

- Hats

no. But what I felt like saying was, 'With what? I'm not your 'bud' and I have no intention of becoming one.'"

Use of Free Time

Watch what everybody else does during breaks. Some of your team members may use that time to work and catch up on things. Others need time alone. Just because you're used to socializing during breaks, don't drop in on them for a chat.

Although asserting your independence and creating a positive, distinctive image are important, you should also make an effort to be on friendly terms with everyone. This will foster productive working relationships at your current job, and you never know when you might end up working with (or for) someone else down the road in your career.

Unofficial Pecking Order

From flow charts and department titles, get familiar with the way authority runs in the office. Most workplaces have an underground pecking order. Observe which people command the most respect. Where do people go when they want advice? Who do they go to get something done in a hurry? In meetings, whom among your coworkers do managers look to first for their ideas and opinions?

Answers to these questions will help you decipher your team's culture.

Unspoken Rules

Steve didn't see a sign forbidding his entrance to the elevator on the right. But as soon as he stepped in, he knew something was wrong. He had been standing with two coworkers, but neither of them followed him into the elevator. He looked at the four people who shared the elevator with him, but none returned his smile.

Steve got off the elevator and waited for his coworkers. When he asked why they hadn't gotten on, one of them said, "That's the executive elevator, Steve." No signs, no instruction book, but part of the company culture nonetheless.

Many offices place great emphasis on recycling and conserving resources. Lisa was embarrassed when she had to be told by her boss that she was being wasteful. She realizes now that she should have noticed what her coworkers were doing for the environment. "I didn't even notice everybody else brought a glass mug for coffee. I just kept using up those styrofoam cups. I figured since someone came in to clean up every night, I didn't have to clean up, too. But my coworkers always did." Lisa learned the hard way that office culture matters.

Today was Juan's birthday. When he arrived at work, many of his coworkers wished him happy birthday.

HOW TO READ BODY LANGUAGE

You can tell a lot about a person's moods, attitude, and personality by his or her body language and gestures. Of course, you should never simply judge a person by his or her body language alone. Be sure to take into account what a person says, the setting you are both in, and your history with the person to make an effective judgment.

- Crossed or folded arms may suggest that a person is either shy or unapproachable or close-minded.

- Hands in pockets can suggest a person is unapproachable or has something to hide.

- Hands covering the mouth can suggest unease, discomfort, or something to hide.

- Pointing can be construed as a reprimand or an aggressive action.

- Hands on hips can convey defensiveness.

- Busy hands (digging in pockets, tapping a pencil, or rubbing body parts) can suggest general unease or nervousness.

- Lack of eye contact can convey meekness or the idea that a person has something to hide.

You can tell a lot about your coworkers' moods and attitudes by reading their body language. (C. Devan/zefa/Corbis)

A few of his closest coworkers even gave him cards and a gift card for Starbucks. This made him especially happy because he was a relatively new employee and wanted to fit in. Later in the week, Juan noticed that a coworker had brought in boxes of donuts and coffee for the office team. Juan asked one of his team members what occasion they were celebrating. He was told that it was the custom of the company for anybody who had a birthday to bring in treats for their coworkers. If someone had only told him this before his birthday, he reasoned to himself, he wouldn't be so embarrassed now.

These examples illustrate just a few of the unspoken rules of the office. Some customs can be detected if you practice reading people's expressions and body language or listen and observe closely what people say and do. Learn to read people so you'll know.

All of us are watchers—of television, of time clocks, of traffic on the freeway—but few are observers. Everyone is looking, not many are seeing.

—Peter Leschak, writer

HIDDEN TRAPS TO AVOID

Do all you can to avoid these hidden traps and unwritten pitfalls:

- *Secret passages.* Take a wrong turn, ally yourself with the wrong person, and you step off the path of success.

- *Closed doors (even when open).* Just because your boss or teammate leaves the door open doesn't mean you can read it as an invitation to walk in whenever you feel like it.

- *Unmarked signals.* Miss the subtle body language of teammates, and you'll commit the same blunders over and over.

- *Misleading signs.* Your boss calls you by your first name, but don't drop your boss' Ms. or Mr. until you're invited to do so.

- *Silent bells.* In many businesses, "nine to five" is just an expression. Get over your school bell mentality and expect to stay after school.

THE WAY THINGS ARE DONE

Ever sit with a small group of friends who hang out together? When an "outsider" sits with you, the atmosphere changes. This new person might talk about things you don't usually talk about. Her slang may be different, and she might miss the

ON THE WEB

Answers.com: Body Language
http://www.answers.com/topic/body-language

Gestures: Body Language and Nonverbal Communication
http://www.csupomona.edu/~tassi/gestures.htm#gestures

What the Boss' Body Language Says
http://hotjobs.yahoo.com/career-articles-what_the_boss_body_language_says-306

meaning of your inside jokes. You might have to explain everything, and she still might not seem to get it.

That's you as the new kid on your team. Henry's father was in the military and moved his family with him for each new assignment. Henry knew what it was like being the new kid, and he used his skills at adapting when he started his own career. Henry talks about his transition to a printing company and his adjustment to his team. "I went to six schools in nine years and got pretty good at reading the way things worked at a school. After the first day, I knew which teachers would be easy, how to steer clear of the principal, which kids I should try to hang with. So when I started working, I just did the same thing. I watched and I listened. It worked out."

☛ FACT

SOP means "standard operating procedure"— the way (policies, regulations, rules) the company operates.

Your first year is the time to accept your team and your team's culture, discern their customs, and adapt.

Be a good detective as you figure out your team's culture. Then nobody will have to say those dreaded words: "That's not the way things are done around here."

If you're the new kid at school, you won't get far by coming in and trying to take over. Your job is to learn how to get along in the new setting.

WHAT NOBODY TELLS YOU, BUT YOU SHOULD KNOW ANYWAY

- Don't talk back to the boss. He's not your professor, looking for a discussion.

- Learn the ropes before you suggest a change.

- Nobody succeeds by clockwatching.

- Allow plenty of time in the morning for problems—traffic, snow, earthquakes, and disasters. There's no such thing as a good excuse.

- New ideas aren't necessarily better.

- Don't talk about your old life, friends, or boss.

- You don't necessarily have the same privileges as everybody else in the office yet.

- Your boss doesn't have to be tactful.

- Your teammates aren't necessarily your buddies.

- Don't dress strangely. Manage your own first impression.

- Job recruiters are never around when you need them—and they exaggerate about job descriptions and responsibilities.

- Your job description is just an outline.

EXAMPLES OF "THE WAY THINGS ARE DONE AROUND HERE"

- Customers and clients are never told about in-house problems.

- Information isn't withheld from teammates in order for an individual to look good.

- We don't go over the boss's head.

- We don't bother the supervisor with details, or we do go over details with the supervisor before acting.

- Executives don't eat (ride elevators, chat, etc.) with new hires.

- Managers aren't contradicted or challenged by their teams when a boss is present.

- Wild behavior at office parties is forbidden.

- Nobody orders alcohol at lunch.

- Never promise customers dates that can't be met.

The same goes for your career. Your first year is the time to accept your team and your team's culture, discern their customs, and adapt. It won't be easy. Most of us spend years trying to find our individuality. You've been struggling to be your own person. Now, in a way, it's time to be theirs. You've been hired by a company to become part of a team. You'll have time later to resurface and more fully

✍ EXERCISE

- List at least five "unwritten rules" of the group you hang out with.

- Pick one of your classes and imagine you're writing a manual entitled "The Way Things Are Done in This Class." What would you be sure to include?

- What are your top-10 expectations as you begin your career? Are any of them not quite realistic?

- How would you dress for the following events?: Graduation, wedding, religious service, family party, field trip, job interview, date. What information would you use to help you decide what is appropriate to wear for each event?

- Learn as much as you can about body language. Has your own body language ever sent out the wrong signal to your parents, friends, or coworkers? If so, work to improve the visual images you send others.

express your individuality. But for now, adapt to the team's style and culture. Make their expectations your expectations.

✔ TRUE OR FALSE: ANSWERS

Do You Understand Team Culture?

1. It's important to learn what your employer expects of you on the job.

True. Many young workers are only concerned with what a company can do for them. But it's important to realize that your boss will have a specific set of expectations for you. Fail to meet these expectations, and you might be shown the door—quickly!

2. I can wear whatever I want to work.

False. It's important to understand and follow the dress code of your company—especially if you're a member of a team. If most of the members of your team wear a suit, then you should, too. By meeting the "dress code" of your team, you are sending a signal to your team members that you are on-board with the project and the company's culture.

3. Learning how to read body language is a key tool for interacting successfully with your team.

True. Body language can tell you if a coworker is happy, upset, tired, bored, shy, nervous, or many other emotions. A cognizance of these moods will help you interact with your coworkers more effectively—even when no one has said a word.

IN SUMMARY . . .

- Your expectations for your new job may be different from reality. Be ready to adjust your expectations based on your actual experiences in the workplace.

- Your job expectations should move from self-focused to team-focused.

- Employers have expectations about you as an individual and as a member of a team. Learning what their spoken and unspoken expectations are is the first step to becoming successful on the job.

- Learn to discern the culture and customs of your team and company.

- Learn the unwritten rules of the workplace by watching and listening to coworkers.

- Try to fit in during your first year on the job. Accept your team's culture and customs and adapt your behavior. There is plenty of time to exercise your individualism once you have more experience on the job.

4

WORLD CUP TEAMS

America is not like a blanket—one piece of unbroken cloth. America is more like a quilt—many patches, many pieces, many colors, many sizes, all woven together by a common thread.

—Rev. Jesse Jackson, civil rights activist

Today's business teams reflect the ethnic makeup of our country. Walk into most businesses and you will probably see men and women from various cultures, ethnic backgrounds, races, and countries. Not everyone on your team will be someone you would have gravitated toward naturally. And yet, you will need to work more closely with these people than with anyone else you know.

Even if your job includes only a few people all fairly similar to you, you can count on the diversity

✔ TRUE OR FALSE?

Are You Ready to Work On a World Cup Team?

1. Many members of my team are from different countries. In order for us to be successful, they need to change their behavior.

2. Not looking someone in the eye while speaking to them is rude.

3. Learning about diverse groups will make me a better person and a stronger member of my team.

Test yourself as you read through this chapter. The answers appear on pages 82–83.

of your customers. In the 21st century, nearly everyone will need to know how to get along with other cultures and races in the workplace. A "World Cup team" is a diverse group of people who know how to work together to win as a team.

WHAT'S THE DIFFERENCE?

Depending on where you went to school, you may have a wealth of multicultural experiences to take with you to your new career. But don't assume that you are prepared just because you went to school with people of other ethnic backgrounds. Attending classes is one thing; working on a team is something else. Teamwork requires depth of understanding and acceptance.

Do you recognize some differences around you at school? Run an inventory on the students you spend most of your free time with. How diverse is your group? Does it reflect your school's diversity, or do you travel only in the circle of people who are most like you?

If you're keeping your distance from other cultures, you may need to rethink. Make an effort now to understand and interact with people who are

The American workplace is becoming increasingly diverse. While you may not become best friends with all of your coworkers, your company's success depends on your ability to get along and work well with people from all backgrounds. (Jose Luis Pelaez, Inc., Corbis)

AMERICAN LABOR FORCE BY RACE, 2006

White	69.1 percent
Hispanic	13.7 percent
Black	11.4 percent
Asian	4.4 percent

Source: U.S. Department of Labor

different from you, and your effort will pay off—now and later. You'll be preparing for a world-class team.

Make an effort now to understand and interact with people who are different from you, and your effort will pay off—now and later.

DIFFERENT DOESN'T MEAN WRONG

What your employer wants is a team of people who, no matter how different they are as individuals, can work together. The first step toward working with diversity is to acknowledge differences. The next step is to accept those differences.

Don't expect to change people from other cultures. It's not your job to mold them to what you consider the correct way of doing things. Instead, expect to learn from others as they learn from you. They may do many things differently, but it doesn't mean they're wrong.

POTENTIAL DIFFERENCES IN TEAM MAKEUP

- Gender
- Race
- Nationality
- Cultural background
- Customs
- Religion
- Financial status (haves and have-nots)
- Education
- Experience
- Level of skill
- Age
- Marital status
- Social life (drinkers/nondrinkers; smokers/nonsmokers; partiers/nonpartiers)

Janelle and Ray worked for the same international company, but held positions in different branches. They ran into the same problem working in multicultural environments. But they handled their situations differently.

At work, the Japanese members on Janelle's team spoke to each other in Japanese, leaving Janelle to wonder what they were talking and laughing about. Because she felt uncomfortable around them, she spent her time developing relationships with the other Americans on her team. After a year, two factions—American and Japanese—had developed in their department. Their team failed to achieve yearly goals and had to restructure.

Every man I meet is my superior in some way. In that, I learn from him.

—Ralph Waldo Emerson, American philosopher

Ray felt the same discomfort on his team as Janelle felt on hers. But after a couple of weeks, he worked up the nerve to ask the Japanese workers if he could talk to them about something. He explains what happened. "I found out that they felt the same way I did, like the Americans were leaving them out. And there were more of us, too. One of the Japanese-Americans said she felt uncomfortable talking in English because she was aware of her accent."

Ray says the Japanese workers continued to speak in Japanese with each other. But after the discussion, everybody made more of an effort to bridge the language gap.

In an ideal workplace, nonnative speakers will have the English-language skills they need to do

READ MORE ABOUT IT

Cox, Taylor, Jr. *Creating the Multicultural Organization: A Strategy for Capturing the Power of Diversity.* San Francisco: Jossey-Bass, 2001.

Dresser, Norine. *Multicultural Manners: Essential Rules of Etiquette for the 21st Century.* Rev. ed. Hoboken, N.J.: Wiley, 2005.

Konrad, Alison M., Pushkala Prasad, and Judith K. Pringle, eds. *Handbook of Workplace Diversity.* Thousand Oaks, Calif.: Sage Publications, 2006.

Mor Barak, Michalle E. *Managing Diversity: Toward a Globally Inclusive Workplace.* Thousand Oaks, Calif.: Sage Publications, 2005.

Samovar, Larry A., Richard E. Porter, and Edwin R. McDaniel. *Intercultural Communication: A Reader.* 12th ed. Florence, Ky.: Wadsworth Publishing, 2008.

Thiederman, Sondra. *Making Diversity Work: 7 Steps for Defeating Bias in the Workplace.* Rev ed. New York: Kaplan Publishing, 2008.

the work required and to develop team relationships. But unless they have to speak English to do the job, it's against the law to force them to converse in English. It's not your job to change them.

ON THE WEB

Diversity Inc.
http://www.diversityinc.com

Equality and Human Rights Commission
http://www.equalityhumanrights.com

Equal Employment Opportunity Commission
http://www.eeoc.gov

Workplace Diversity
http://www.workplacediversity.com

Instead, be honest, be friendly, and respect their language.

Language may be the most obvious cultural difference. But it's just the beginning.

Remember that outward differences just show the tip of the iceberg. All you see is a coworker who won't work on Saturday. Another refuses to work on Sunday. But behind those outward differences lie deep-seated beliefs, values, attitudes, and expectations.

America is a true melting pot, with people from hundreds of countries making up corporate teams. The way people do things, from eye contact and personal space to handshakes and other greetings, can vary greatly by country—even in our increasing global world. Consider these examples of differing customs and behaviors, from the book *CultureGrams* (Ann Arbor, Mich.: ProQuest, 2008), before you judge classmates and coworkers from other countries.

- In Afghanistan (and other predominantly Muslim countries) men do not usually shake hands with women.

- In Japan, "shaking one hand from side to side with the palm forward means 'no.'"

- In the Republic of Chad, a person agrees by clicking their tongue against their palate and moving their chin upward quickly.

- In Bulgaria, agreement is "indicated by shaking the head from side to side," and "no is expressed with one or two nods."

- In Peru, people stand very close together when talking.

All your people skills need to come into play for intercultural team relationships. Eileen kept a notebook of observations when she was a foreign exchange student in France during her junior year of high school. Her habit of noticing, adapting to, and accepting people made Eileen's career transition easier.

Eileen, now a buyer for a large department store, explains: "My supervisor here thinks I can get along with anybody. For example, I've noticed which cultures like handshakes. With French clients, I extend my hand when we meet and when I leave. Other clients [from other countries] are more comfortable doing business after a huge lunch during which nobody talks business. I do what makes the client comfortable."

Goal Oriented versus People Oriented

One way to understand differences is to recognize how you look at success and identity. Although

POTENTIAL CULTURAL DIFFERENCES

- Language
- Food
- Manners
- Holidays
- Physical mannerisms
- Concept of personal space (what's mine/yours/ours)
- Ethics
- Values
- Family
- Ownership
- Time
- Dress

some Americans are more goal oriented and others people oriented, as a nation we tend to be goal oriented. Ours is a culture of "doing," rather than a culture of "being."

It is the individual who is not interested in his fellow men who has the greatest difficulties in life and provides the greatest injury to others. It is from among such individuals that all human failures spring.

—Alfred Adler, psychologist

CHARACTERISTIC DIFFERENCES IN THE WAY WE THINK

Goal Oriented	People Oriented
Self-worth comes from achieving	Self-worth comes from relationships
Time is tightly scheduled	Time is relative
Individualism is vital	Need to belong
Future oriented	Bound to past
Needs change	Seeks stability
Immediate family is important	Extended family vital
Likes measurable goals	Wants people to agree

ARE YOU READY FOR GLOBAL EMPLOYMENT?

Did you know that showing the sole of your shoe to others is an insult in many Middle Eastern countries? That being too touchy-feely in Denmark is a no-no? That the French signify "OK" by using the thumbs-up sign? That people in Thailand consider it impolite to talk with your hands or place them in your pockets as you speak? Cultural variations such as these exist all over the world, and if you plan to work abroad, you will need to master the cultural ins and outs of the nation where you live and work. Here are a few tips to consider as you prepare to work abroad:

- *A little research goes a long way.* Before you go, read about the country and its culture in books and on the Internet. Talk with people who have lived or worked in the country. If you are still in school, consider studying abroad to learn more about other cultures.

- *Learn the language.* Learn at least the basics ("hello," "goodbye," "please," "thank you") before you go. Take a short 8-10 week course covering language basics. Purchase language software to brush up on your language skills at home.

- *Take an international etiquette training course.* Such courses are increasingly becoming popular as more companies expand globally. In fact, 62 percent of business executives and 82 percent of administrative professionals polled by OfficeTeam in 2008 said they would benefit from taking an international etiquette course.

- *Be cognizant of cultural/religious holidays.* Avoid scheduling business trips or appointments during culturally sensitive times such as Ramadan in the Islamic world.

- *Embrace the culture.* Immerse yourself in the country's culture. Ask your coworkers to help your learn about their country's food, music, arts, sports, traditions, etc.

- *Hold that thought.* Don't act like an expert on the country's history, culture, religion, or relationships with its neighbors. For example, if you work in China, you should probably avoid discussing human rights abuses, pollution, substandard goods, and any other potentially touchy topics. Discuss only safe topics such as sports, weather, and work issues.

(*CultureGrams*; *Pink* magazine; *Chicago Tribune*)

You'll encounter many cultural differences in your career. Learn from them.

What do you ask when you first meet someone? "Where do you go to school?" "What jobs have you had?" "What do you want to do when you graduate?"

Or are your questions more like these: "Tell me about your family." "Did you grow up around here?" "What's it like living where you live?"

The first set of questions is more goal oriented. What do you do? The second set centers on people. Who are you? If you met someone of Slavic descent, for example, you might get to know that person fairly well before you are asked about your job. Americans usually ask job-related questions in the first five minutes. Americans tend to be competitive. But in Africa, home of some of the greatest runners in the world, many people race for fun, waiting at the finish line so all can cross together.

You'll run across many cultural differences in your career. Learn from them. Different doesn't mean wrong.

PLAYING FAIR

Eileen, the buyer who spent a year as a foreign exchange student, says there's a trick to fair play in dealing with other cultures. She says, "I've never met anybody who didn't think they were meeting the other person halfway. But what looks like 50-50 to you never looks like 50-50 to the other guy." We have to go out of our way to help other people feel like part of the team.

FIVE KEYS TO FAIR PLAY

1. Be a help, not a critic.

2. Don't expect someone from another culture to know all about yours. Try to learn all you can about theirs.

3. Don't jump to conclusions based on stereotypes. (That's why he's late. That's why she's emotional.)

4. Be alert for gender and culture concerns.

5. Build bridges of understanding and respect. (Your career may depend on it.)

Someone who has an attitude of fair play doesn't think, "That guy doesn't even know that we don't do that kind of thing here." Instead, the difference is seen and accepted: "In his country (or neighborhood) that's one of the things people do." Remember, until you're the boss, it's not your job to change people or demand they change. Your job is to get along and respect your team.

PREPARING FOR THE MULTICULTURAL ENVIRONMENT

How can you get ready to function on your multi-cultural team? Take advantage of the opportunities around you. Take a foreign language. Find a pen pal in another country and try to learn about another culture. Get involved in an international club for high school or college students. Host or invite foreign students into your home for holidays or hospitality. Join a volunteer organization that serves other cultures. Join a church, mosque, temple, or community-outreach program.

Talk. Men and women have different points of view on many things. Try to understand. Ask questions.

If there's a student with a disability in your school, get to know her. If you feel awkward talking while looking down at someone in a wheelchair, tell that person. Be honest. Honesty is the start of understanding and being understood.

DID YOU KNOW?

The American workforce is becoming increasingly diverse. The number of Asian workers in the U.S. workforce is expected to increase 30 percent by 2016, the number of Hispanic workers is expected to increase by 30 percent by 2016, and the number of African-American workers is expected to increase by 16 percent.

Source: U.S. Department of Labor

Want to be on a World Cup team? Start now to broaden your understanding of the world. The more people you can get along with now, the smoother your transition is likely to be when you join your work team.

Want to be on a World Cup team? Start now to broaden your understanding of the world.

✍ EXERCISE

Try some of these exercises to sharpen your point of view and help you see things from someone else's point of view.

- Think of the last time you argued with someone. Write the argument as if you're the other person. What are you (as this other person) trying to say? What are your thoughts when you're not being understood?

- When was the last time you felt terribly out of place? Write down what it felt like. What made it worse? Better?

- Imagine you come from another racial background. How do you feel when you're around a group of laughing students of a different race?

Continued on page 82

Continued from page 81

- Learn more about another country by reading books, surfing the Internet, eating at a restaurant that serves the foreign country's cuisine, attending a cultural event, talking with an individual from that country, or even visiting the country with friends or a school group. Compare and contrast your country with the country that you are interested in. Basic comparisons/contrasts could involve food, greetings, gestures, language, clothing styles, religions, and customs.

✔ TRUE OR FALSE: ANSWERS

Are You Ready to Work On a World Cup Team?

1. Many members of my team are from different countries. In order for us to be successful, they need to change their behavior.

False. Your job is not to change your coworkers, but to find ways to transcend cultural differences to ensure team success.

2. Not looking someone in the eye while speaking to them is rude.

False. Americans often consider those who do not make eye contact as aloof, unconfident, or having something to hide. But this isn't true in all cultures. Some Asian cultures actually consider excessive eye contact to be rude! This is why it is never good to generalize when it comes to cultural traditions—especially in our increasingly diverse work world. It's better to study each group's culture to learn what is socially acceptable and unacceptable.

3. Learning about diverse groups will make me a better person and a stronger member of my team.

True. America is a melting pot and a world leader because of its constant infusion of different cultures and perspectives. Learning to interact with people from other cultures, religions, etc. will broaden your horizons and make you a better team player.

IN SUMMARY . . .

- The business world is becoming an increasingly diverse place. You will work with people from various cultures, ethnic backgrounds, races, and even countries. You may not naturally gravitate toward these coworkers, but it is exceedingly important that you establish a good working relationship with them.

- In the workplace, not only will you work with people from different cultural and ethnic backgrounds; you will work with people of different genders, religions, education levels, ages, financial statuses, marital statuses, and social experiences. Accepting people who have different life experiences from you is the first step toward being part of a World Cup team.

- Your job is not to change members of your team who have different backgrounds. Your job to get along with them and work as part of a team.

- Remember that coworkers from other countries may have customs and behaviors (greetings, eye contact, personal space) different from yours. Be observant to learn about these differences.

- It is important to remember that Americans are generally considered to be goal oriented (or a culture of "doing"), rather than people oriented (or a culture of "being") like many other nations. Keep these differences in mind when you work with team members who come from different countries.

- Observe the Five Keys to Fair Play when dealing with coworkers from different backgrounds.

- Take advantage of opportunities to learn more about different people of all types. It will help you become a stronger teammate and a better human being.

5

TEAM CONFLICTS AND OTHER CONCERNS

One widely used appraiser for new employees stresses these job-performance factors:

- Works effectively in groups

- Resolves team conflicts

- Works with other departments

- Establishes and maintains cooperative working relationships

- Is flexible and open-minded, focusing on team efforts

No matter where you work, getting along with your coworkers, the members of your team, will be one of your most important duties. You can't just change "groups" or decide not to play as you may have when you were younger. There's no semester break, no change of class and teacher. This is your team, and you have to learn to get along.

☞ FACT

According to the HRD Press (http://www.hrdpress.com), conflict over facts is the easiest to resolve, and conflict over values is the most difficult to resolve.

An understanding of basic personalities can help us appreciate where other people are coming from.

PERSONALITY TYPES

Have you ever run up against someone who rubbed you the wrong way? You just couldn't seem to get along. Not your type, you decided. Although it's never a good idea to box people into convenient types, an understanding of basic personalities can help us appreciate where other people are coming

FOUR PERSONALITY TYPES

Sanguine
Outgoing
Popular
Life of the party
Lives for fun

Melancholy
Artistic
Close friendships
Organized
Analytical

Choleric
Leader
Confident
Forceful
Goal oriented

Phlegmatic
Easygoing
Gets along with all
Balanced
Steady

from. If we can understand them, we may be able to avoid some personality conflicts.

One system of classifying personality types is according to temperaments. Four distinct temperaments, or personality types, were identified by Hippocrates more than 2,000 years ago: sanguine, melancholy, choleric, and phlegmatic.

- *Sanguines* are fun, outgoing people who enjoy an audience and all the attention they can get. Their strengths usually lie in public speaking, being at ease with a variety of people, and a readiness to take risks and try new things.

- *Melancholics* are more introspective, deep thinkers. They tend to be artistic and are capable of deep friendships. They can be well organized and analytical.

- *Cholerics* are born leaders, and they know it. They are confident, usually goal-oriented, and capable. You can count on them to follow through with their plans and lead the charge toward goals.

- *Phlegmatics* are easygoing and likeable. They seem to get along with everybody and keep themselves and life in balance. They can adjust well to most circumstances and people.

DEALING WITH DIFFERENT PERSONALITIES

Imagine that you spend a week observing the members of your team and conclude Sam is a sanguine; Mary, a melancholic; Carl, a choleric; and Fran, a phlegmatic. (Hopefully you won't put your teammates in such tight boxes. Few people fit 100 percent into a single personality type. So, just imagine these coworkers for the sake of illustration.) What conflicts should you watch out for? If you have an idea what to expect, you can act, not react. Also, what needs can you anticipate and help meet for each member?

If you have an idea what to expect, you can act, not react.

Sam Sanguine

Sam Sanguine is so friendly that you probably can't imagine coming into conflict with him. However, don't overlook the fact that Sam always needs to be the center of attention. Here are some potential conflicts you might have with Sam:

- If you are also a sanguine, you may represent competition to Sam. He may become jealous of you or even begin to resent it if you steal the spotlight. If this happens, don't react. Let Sam have the applause, and just do your job.

- If you're not a sanguine, you may tire of Sam's need to entertain. Try to have patience with Sam and realize that he doesn't mean any harm.

- Sam may not want to get serious when you're ready to get down to business. He'll infringe on your privacy, stopping by your desk for a chat while you're in the middle of an important project. Be careful how you explain your need to get on with your work.

What needs will Sam have? If you meet someone like Sam, being aware of these needs will reduce the chances of personality conflicts.

- Sam needs your attention. It doesn't cost you anything, so go ahead and give it.

- Sam needs your approval. Compliment his ideas occasionally and laugh at his jokes if you think they're funny. Be careful how you disagree with him.

- Sam may not realize it, but he could use help being consistent. He may drive your team crazy by showing up late for meetings or forgetting the agenda. Ask him if he'd like a copy of your notes, and remind him of meeting times. Minimizing conflict will help your team and it will help you.

Teamwork is essential to setting goals, resolving conflicts, and achieving desired results. People do not work on an 'island.' Communication and collaboration amongst team members is important for each company, department, or group to grow stronger. Building on strengths and weaknesses, strategizing, and brainstorming are cornerstones to an innovative group looking for creative solutions. By developing strong skills in the confines of a team, you can achieve greater success.

—Cathy Cortez, senior manager-labor relations, Canadian National Railway Company

Melancholy Mary

Melancholy Mary is always organized and working hard. She doesn't slack on responsibilities, and she stays focused on her work. So what kind of conflict could you run into with Mary?

- Because Mary tends to be a perfectionist, she'll likely get upset if you're not orderly and disciplined, too. Understand that her standards are high and that you may never do well enough to please her, since no one is perfect.

- Mary's perfectionism can make her negative. She may find the downside to every team project. Don't get drawn into her negativism or depression.

- Mary's feelings are easily hurt. Be sensitive, and don't joke at her expense. If you offend her, apologize. She can hold a grudge.

Since melancholics can get depressed, stay positive with them.

A successful team is a group of many hands but of one mind.

—Bill Bethel

What needs could you try to help Mary fulfill?

- Mary needs to be drawn out. Ask her for her opinion and try to talk to her about her interests.

- Do your best to meet her need for order and discipline. Don't be late for meetings, and keep schedules to stay organized.

- Mary doesn't treat relationships lightly, so be careful not to treat your relationship with her lightly either. Keep in mind what things and people are important to her.

- Mary needs some time alone. Be sensitive to her desire to work rather than talk.

- Since melancholics can get depressed, stay positive with them. Don't scold Mary, but encourage her by pointing out how well she's doing.

Carl Choleric

Carl Choleric is very focused on your team's goals, so you probably expect that he'll be dedicated and easy to work with. However, there are a few traits in his personality type that may cause conflict:

- Carl honestly believes he's right and you're wrong. Arguing with him probably won't get you much more than a fight. Be diplomatic and don't buck his authority unless necessary.

- Carl expects you to work as hard as he does to reach goals. Work hard. Don't procrastinate. Follow through with your responsibilities.

- Understand that Carl is more focused on team goals than on team members. Don't be offended by his bark or his apparent lack of interest in you as a person. Don't take his criticism personally. It's just his way.

Carl may seem so confident that he doesn't have any needs, but he does.

- Carl needs to succeed. Do all you can to make your team (and Carl) look good.

- Carl may step on team members' toes and not even know it. You may be able to follow along and smooth feathers from time to time, reminding others that Carl doesn't mean everything he says.

- On occasion, you might need to confront Carl. He can take it. He may not see your point of view, but you may need to try and show him.

Fran Phlegmatic

Fran Phlegmatic is laid back and easy to get along with. Her well-balanced personality allows her to get along with everyone, but after a time, personality conflicts can surface.

- Fran is so easygoing that she may slip into laziness. When she doesn't do her part on a team project, you may resent her. Instead, accept her, but offer to help her meet her objectives.

- Because Fran seeks peace above all else, she probably won't volunteer for extra duties or take risks for the team. You may get frustrated waiting for her to get off her duff and get going. Instead, think of ways you can challenge her to act.

How can you meet Fran's needs?

- Don't be argumentative with her. Help her keep the peace.

- When you see a job you're sure she'd be good for, encourage her to volunteer. Help her determine a plan of action.

- Understand that Fran may be hiding her problems. She'd rather live with dissatisfaction than risk a conflict. Be sensitive enough to figure out what Fran's hiding.

DREADED BEHAVIOR TYPES

No matter how aware you are, there are certain behavior types you're bound to clash with sooner or later.

Being aware of the different temperaments, or personality types, can reduce the number of team conflicts you get drawn into needlessly. But no matter how aware you are, there are certain behavior types you're bound to run into sooner or later. In fact, after you read about the four types (worst enemy, bum, child, tattletale), you'll probably think of people you already know who fit these descriptions. At school, you can usually just avoid these people. But if they're on your team, you'll need to know how to handle them. And, most important, never behave like one of these types yourself.

FOUR DREADED BEHAVIOR TYPES

Type	Defense Against
Worst Enemy	Keep records, send memos, confront
Bum	Offer to help, work hard yourself
Child	Offer alternate times for talk
Tattletale	Tell little about yourself

The way to develop the best that is in a man is by appreciation and encouragement.

—Charles Schwab, early 20th-century
business leader

Your Worst Enemy

Your worst enemy on the job can take many forms: male, female, young, old, any personality type. She may want your job. He may want you to look bad.

You may or may not have helped make this person your worst enemy.

Andrea had never had a worst enemy until she began working as a trainee for a telephone company. It took her about three months to catch on. "This woman started by making fun of me to other trainees behind my back. I tried to laugh it off. But when I found out she'd told the supervisor I wasn't working out, I knew I had to do something to defend myself. The supervisor asked me how committed I was to my job, why I was late, and left early. And it wasn't true."

Andrea's solution was to keep good records. "I told the supervisor I hadn't left early, but I didn't know if she believed me. From then on I kept detailed records on my calendar. I sent memos about projects. The next time I talked with my supervisor, I was armed."

An opponent is someone whose strength joined to yours creates a certain result.

—Sadaharu Oh, Japanese baseball player

Many worst enemies are deceivers. One approach is a direct confrontation. If you decide to confront, be specific. Don't blame. Instead of saying, "I think you're out to make me look bad," wait for a clear issue. "I was told by the supervisor that you reported I came in late last week. I have a record that in fact I came in early every day last week. I don't understand."

Memos to all team members, including your enemy, can make a good defense against accusations that you're not doing enough work. Make copies of everything you do.

Don't go over your enemy's head without informing him or her. Stay aboveboard so that none of the accusations will have a foundation. As long as you keep doing the right thing, others will see it. Don't try to force your team to take sides or choose between you and your enemy.

Don't try to force your team to take sides or choose between you and your enemy.

CONFLICT IS NOT AWAYS BAD

According to researchers at the University of Illinois (http://www.vta.spcomm.uiuc.edu), conflict in the workplace can actually be beneficial. Here's how:

- *It improves the group's situation.* Conflict forces team members to face possible defects in a solution and thus produce better answers.

- *Workers are more productive.* Instead of trying to avoid conflict and becoming distant, team members can concentrate on the task at hand.

- *It is a stress reliever.* By getting a conflict out in the open, group members are given a chance to vent their emotions and release tensions. Once the conflict is resolved, the group members may even grow closer.

- *It changes the organization of the group.* By acknowledging a conflict, group members may discover what they are truly best suited to do.

The Bum

By now you've worked on enough group projects in school, on a team, or in a club to know there's bound to be someone on your team who doesn't carry his weight. What do you do when this happens on your team? How do you handle the bum who makes more work for you and everybody else because he doesn't keep up his end?

Megan hated group papers and projects in high school. "I always ended up doing the whole thing, or I got a lower grade because my partner didn't do her end." She didn't think she'd have an easy adjustment working on a team of librarians in a city library. After a week on the job, Megan recognized the same "bum" type in one of her team members, Robert. Luckily, she discovered her employers already had a built-in way to handle the problem.

Laziness grows on people; it begins in cobwebs and ends in iron chains. The more one has to do, the more he is able to accomplish.

—Thomas Buxton, British writer
and social activist

"We all signed a contract that included a team clause saying we were committed to working together as a team and sharing responsibilities and work. Our team leader had us come up with a list of things we expected from each other. One of the expectations was that everybody would do his share. So when Robert didn't, we all felt it. First, we asked him how we could help him make his commitment. We did his work for him sometimes, but we didn't cover for him. And after awhile, he was let go."

Usually, if you keep doing what you need to do, the bum won't last. Give him enough rope, and he'll trip himself up.

The Child

The "child," also known as the "baby," hasn't grown up enough to act like a professional. She brings personal problems to the office and wants you and everybody else to take care of her. If you let her, the child will waste your work time telling you the sordid details of her love life. Her feelings are so easily hurt, you may be afraid to tell her you don't have time to talk.

How do you handle the needy child? If you tell her exactly what you think, she probably can't handle it. You may make the conflict worse and affect your relationship with her and the functioning of your team. On the other hand, if you say nothing, she'll drain you.

Maturity is knowing when to be immature.

—Randall Hall, American musician

Gretchen had a "child" on her shift in retail sales. Every free moment, the other woman latched on to Gretchen to pour out her latest personal trauma. "I couldn't just tell her to stop talking to me," Gretchen said. "So I started offering her other times."

Gretchen tried to word her requests politely and warmly: "So we don't miss a customer, let's save our talk for the next break." Or, "I'd like to hear this, but I'm afraid I won't be able to focus. Would you like to go out to lunch Friday and tell me about it then?"

You have to be careful not to hurt a child's feelings, but you can't get drawn into being his therapist. Be the adult—the tactful adult.

The Tattletale

The tattletale loves to be the bearer of juicy news. He knows everything about everybody in the office, and he loves to spread the word. How do you handle the tattletale?

Keep your personal life personal, and refuse to gossip about others.

First, if the news he's spreading is about you, then you know not to tell him anything not for public broadcast. The less you tell him about yourself, the less ammunition he can have against you.

If he chooses to tattle or gossip to you about other people, be polite, but don't buy into the revelation. If you're not impressed or interested, he will probably not waste his time on you. If he continues, it's better to handle him with questions than to accuse. "And you saw her do that?" you could ask innocently. Again, do the right thing yourself. Keep your personal life personal, and refuse to gossip about others.

CHOOSE YOUR BATTLES CAREFULLY

Do all you can to avoid team conflicts through understanding and acting, rather than reacting. But if nothing short of direct confrontation works, be sure you pick your fights carefully.

Employers don't put up with in-house fighting. For your own sake, save your complaints for

✍ EXERCISE

- What personality type or types best describe you? Why?

- Think of two people you have trouble getting along with. What personality types do you think they are? Write down three ways that you might try to handle them.

- Do you know any people who might fit the descriptions of the worst enemy, bum, child, or tattletale? What have you done to try to get along with them?

Winning an argument or a battle may feel good for a minute, but you're going to have to put up with a sore loser for a long time.

the majors. Minor irritations aren't worth a fight. Be prepared to be patient, to give more than you receive, and to do more than your fair share. Andrea endured a lot of snide remarks from her "worst enemy" before confronting her and involving the supervisor.

Here lies the body of William Jay,
Who died maintaining his right of way—
He was right, dead right, as he sped along,
But he's just as dead as if he were wrong.

—from the *Boston Transcript*

Plan your "fights." Don't get drawn into one through anger or frustration. Present your case logically, rationally, and honestly. Keep the argument pointed at issues, rather than individuals. Try saying, "It didn't get done," rather than "You didn't do it."

DID YOU KNOW?

Sexual harassment can happen to anyone. In *Oncale v. Sundowner Offshore Services*, which was decided in 1998, same-sex harassment and harassment of males was recognized as unlawful.

Finally, whenever possible, give the other person a way out, a way to save face. Winning an argument or a battle may feel good for a minute, but you're going to have to put up with a sore loser for a long time. Don't lose a relationship just to get your way on one issue.

SEXUAL HARASSMENT: A SERIOUS WORKPLACE CONCERN

In this chapter, we have described and offered solutions to several basic conflicts that occur in the workplace. In addition to these problems and annoyances, there is a considerably more serious concern that may occur in the workplace—sexual harassment. The term *sexual harassment* was coined in 1978 when the federal Equal Employment Opportunity Commission set guidelines to regulate it. The issue of sexual harassment is taken very seriously today. This is illustrated in the case of Jeremy.

Jeremy was the life of every party in high school. Girls were dying to go out with him. Jeremy knew enough not to tell flat-out dirty jokes at the office, but he was quick with the one-liner—the sexual innuendo that could make a girl blush. After two weeks on the job, Jeremy was called into the personnel office. Two women had complained of sexual harassment.

The law defines sexual harassment as any unwelcome sexual advances or requests for sexual favors or any conduct of a sexual nature when:

- Submission is made explicitly or implicitly a term or condition of initial or continued employment.

- Submission or rejection is used as a basis of working conditions including promotion, salary adjustment, assignment of work, or termination.

- Such conduct has the purpose or effect of substantially interfering with an individual's work environment or creating an intimidating, hostile, or offensive work environment.

SEVEN WAYS TO KEEP SEXUAL HARASSMENT OUT OF THE WORKPLACE

1. Don't make crude jokes.

2. Don't laugh at crude jokes.

3. Be careful about teasing others.

4. Watch the way you word compliments. ("That's an attractive dress," rather than "That's a sexy dress" or "You look hot!")

5. Don't repeatedly ask a coworker out if he or she displays no interest in joining you.

6. Stick with "hi" and a handshake, rather than the hello-or-goodbye hug or kiss.

7. Don't repeatedly and obviously exclude individuals from discussions and activities.

☛ FACT

In Fiscal Year 2007, the Equal Employment
Opportunity Commission (EEOC) received
12,510 charges of sexual harassment—males
filed approximately 16 percent of these charges.
The EEOC recovered $49.9 million in monetary
benefits for charging parties and other aggrieved
individuals (this total does not include monetary
benefits obtained through litigation).

Most companies try to come up with a clearer
definition of sexual harassment. Gorman-Rupp, an
international manufacturing company, expands the
policy:

> Sexual harassment is unlawful . . . . All
> employees have the right to expect a work-
> place which is free of conduct that is of
> a harassing or abusive nature. Offensive
> employee behavior also includes physical

USEFUL RESOURCES

The EEOC offers a variety of publications about
discrimination and sexual harassment at its Web site,
http://www.eeoc.gov/publications.html. Many of
these are available for electronic download; others are
available as print publications.

U.S. MERIT SYSTEMS PROTECTION BOARD

The U.S. Merit Systems Protection Board conducts studies on sexual harassment in the federal workplace. To learn more, visit http://www.mspb.gov.

WHAT TO DO IF YOU HAVE BEEN SEXUALLY HARASSED

If you are the victim of sexual harassment, don't put up with it. You don't have to. First, talk to the person or people involved and clearly tell them you consider their actions and attitude sexually harassing. Ask them to stop. If they don't, inform them that you are serious and plan to take your official complaint to the company through the proper channels. Then do it. If your boss won't take you seriously, see your company's human resources representative or a good lawyer. If your problem is still not resolved, consider contacting the Equal Employment Opportunity Commission (http://www.eeoc.gov), a federal agency that oversees federal harassment and discrimination laws.

advances or intimidations, sexual or otherwise, and uninvited suggestive remarks. Any employee who joins in or condones harassment or abuse of another employee shall also be liable for discipline.

SURF THE WEB: WORKPLACE CONFLICTS AND CONCERNS

Association for Conflict Resolution
http://www.acrnet.org

Center for Conflict Resolution
http://www.ccrchicago.org

Conflict Information Consortium
http://conflict.colorado.edu

Harassment Hotline Inc.
http://www.end-harassment.com

Institute for Conflict Analysis and Resolution
http://icar.gmu.edu

Online Journal of Peace and Conflict Resolution
http://www.trinstitute.org/ojpcr

Women's Rights at Work
http://www.citizenactionny.org

WorkRelationships Inc.
http://www.workrelationships.com

Note the phrases "uninvited suggestive remarks" and "any employee who joins in." Work is not the place for Jeremy's innuendos. What you say and how you say it may be interpreted as suggestive. There have been harassment cases filed against senators, business managers, professors, construction workers, and students, and these allegations are no joke. Whether or not someone files a suit against you, you will be hurting your team and wrecking your own career if you engage in such activity.

✔ TRUE OR FALSE: ANSWERS

Do You Know How to Get Along with Your Coworkers?

1. Conflict among team members is inevitable.

True. Put two people in a room together, and they will eventually disagree about something. This is even more true for a large group of people from varied backgrounds. What's most important is that group members treat conflict as a means to improve the project and foster constructive debate—not as a way to settle petty scores or otherwise derail the success of the project.

2. Men cannot be sexually harassed.

False. In 2007, approximately 16 percent of sexual harassment claims filed with the Equal

Employment Opportunity Commission were filed by men.

3. It's better not to complain to your bosses when sexually harassed by a coworker or boss.

False. Sexual harassment is wrong and should never be tolerated. Always speak up so the situation can be remedied.

IN SUMMARY . . .

- Understanding the four main personality types will help you appreciate where other people are coming from at work.

- Pick your fights carefully at work. It is often wisest to avoid confrontation if possible.

- Conflict among team members is inevitable. You can do your best to avoid it, however, by remaining flexible and open-minded.

- The four dreaded personality types that you may encounter in the workplace are worst enemy, bum, child, and tattletale.

- In order to avoid team conflicts, be cooperative and do your part—no one likes a lazy teammate.

- Sexual harassment is a serious workplace issue. To ensure that it doesn't happen in your office, don't make crude/inappropriate jokes or laugh with anyone who does.

- If you are sexually harassed, tell the person or people involved that you consider their actions and attitude sexually harassing. If this doesn't remedy the problem, talk to your company's human resource department, a good lawyer, or the Equal Employment Opportunity Commission.

6

TEAM GOAL SETTING AND NEGOTIATING

G oals come in all sizes. Every day you set certain goals and try to meet them. Some goals you work hard for; others are more like wishes.

On school mornings, you probably have a goal to get to class on time. To reach your goal, you break the task down into small steps, or objectives, such as get up, eat breakfast, dress, and get to school.

Your goal is to get to school on time, which is 8:05 A.M. If you're organized, you set your alarm for 6:30. Next, you give yourself 20 minutes for breakfast. To reach that objective, you have a system: Grab spoon and bowl in one hand, milk and cereal in the other.

You need 30 minutes in the bathroom. However, experience tells you that you may run into trouble. Your sister also needs 30 minutes, and you share the same bathroom. You have several contingency

✔ TRUE OR FALSE?

Do You Know How to Set Goals and Negotiate?

1. Team goals should be precise and match the overall goals of my company.

2. You can still meet goals as a team even if half the members aren't contributing.

3. Teamwork requires constant negotiation.

Test yourself as you read through this chapter. The answers appear on pages 131–132.

plans: Cut five minutes off breakfast, turn off your sister's alarm, or just beat her in the mad dash down the hall to claim first dibs on the bathroom.

The rest of the morning has been broken down into dressing time and getting to school. With those objectives reached, you walk into school at 8:04. You reached your goal.

However, if you had not set clear goals and objectives, the story would have a different ending. Sure, you'd like to get to school on time, but you didn't think to set an alarm. Mom yells to wake you up, but you drift back to sleep. When you finally get downstairs to eat breakfast, you're too sleepy to know what time it is. To top it off, your sister beat you to the bathroom and won't surface for hours. You wear the clothes you wore yesterday, but you're still too late to catch the bus. It's second period when you walk into school. What's worse, you're still not sure what made you late.

Goals and objectives are a part of everyday life. When you become a member of a work team, you will need to know how to participate in setting goals. Those goals and objectives will determine everything your team does.

DEFINING YOUR MAIN GOAL

It's the stuff of comedy movies: A promising, but nervous, high school freshman is eager to make his debut on his school's football team. Finally his moment comes. He intercepts a pass, runs for all he's worth, and crosses the goal line—the wrong goal line. He reaches the goal, but it is the wrong goal.

We dream about where we want to go, but we don't have a map to get there. What is the map? In essence, the written word. What is the difference between a dream and a goal? Once again, the written word.

—**Gene Donohue,** *Goal Setting: Powerful Written Goals in 7 Easy Steps* (http://www.topachievement.com/ goalsetting.html)

The goals your team sets have to align with the company's stated and unstated goals.

The first step in setting team goals is to define the main goal. Underlying any goals your team sets is the company goal. Your company will have a statement of purpose or a mission statement. Make sure you understand what it says, and what it doesn't.

John's first job was selling retail goods in a hardware store. He assumed that his employer's main goal was to sell more products and make more money. John pressed every sale, making sure most customers left with something. However, the hardware store relied on returning, faithful clientele. John's customers may have left with purchases, but some of the customers never returned. Needless to say, John got called into his boss' office.

After you read your employer's mission statement, talk to team members. Ask them what they think are the unstated goals of the organization. The goals your team sets have to align with the company's stated and unstated goals.

CLEARLY STATE YOUR GOAL

Assume the higher management of an automobile manufacturer has asked all departments to come up with a main goal. The production department came up with this: "To increase production of parts." Higher management sent the department back to the drawing board. Why? Though the department's goal fit perfectly with the stated and unstated goals of the company, it wasn't specific enough.

A good goal has to be specific and measurable. How would the company's production team know exactly when their goal was met? When they produced one more part than the current rate? How long did they have to meet the goal? The department's final, acceptable goal clearly stated: "To increase the hourly production of parts from 23 to 30 by November 1." Management was satisfied because the goal included a specific date and number.

When making goals, visualize all necessary steps. What will the achievement of your goal look like? For example, assume you are a member of a service club. Your goal is to fundraise for charities. Which organization are you focusing on? Is your goal to raise money for a local charity or to get food to Africa? The answer affects your team's strategy. Will you only try to get cash contributions, or will you go for donations of food? Do you need to plan how to convert your cash into food? You won't know all these answers unless your club's fundraising goal is clearly stated. Get it in writing. The clearer the vision of where you're going, the easier it will be to get there.

The clearer the vision of where you're going, the easier it will be to get there.

If you fail to plan, you plan to fail.

—Anonymous

INVOLVE THE WHOLE TEAM

A strong team makes sure every member has a chance to help form goals. The trend in business is to empower teams with more authority. The logic is simple. The more involved you are in forming a goal, the more you have at stake to see it fulfilled.

First, take personal responsibility for your team's goals. Be prepared to contribute in meetings. Make positive suggestions, rather than shooting down other people's ideas. Just as in your classes, if you do some research and preliminary planning, you'll have something to add to discussions.

Next, take responsibility for making your team pull together. (It's something every team member should do, even new members.) If Larry, one of your team members, is shy, ask for his opinion on your given project. If he has a good idea, say so. If he is more comfortable talking one-on-one, talk to him individually. Then, during your next team meeting, you can help get him started, saying something like "Larry had a good idea about the project." In other words, do whatever it takes to get the most out of your teammates—and out of yourself.

Alone we can do so little; together we can do so much.

—Helen Keller, American author and activist

BREAK THE GOAL INTO OBJECTIVES

Once the team has a clear goal, it's time to divide it into smaller goals or objectives. Once each objective is achieved, you should reach your main goal.

SURF THE WEB: SETTING GOALS

About Goal Setting: The 20-Minute Tutorial
   http://www.about-goal-setting.com

eHow: How to Set Goals
   http://www.ehow.com/how_2048963_set-goals.
   html

Goal Setting: Powerful Written Goals in 7 Easy Steps
   http://www.topachievement.com/goalsetting.html

Goal Setting for Everyone
   http://www.mygoals.com

Personal Goal Setting: Planning to Live Life Your
Own Way
   http://www.mindtools.com/page6.html

Setting Goals
   http://www.xsitepro.com/Setting-Goals.pdf

At the University of Missouri, a group of six students set a common goal: to introduce pass/fail classes at the university by the beginning of fall enrollment. The goal was thoroughly discussed, then written clearly. They called themselves STEP (Student Team for Educational Progress).

The team had to come up with objectives that would lead to their main goal. Students met for a brainstorming session and came up with over 70 strategies to get pass/fail classes on campus. Many of the brainstorming ideas were impractical or silly, such as staging a sit-in at Jesse Hall, delivering brownies with information on STEP to the trustees, and kidnapping the registrar (a joke, to be sure). Several more effective ideas won a consensus of support. They could get students to sign a petition. They should research other universities that use a pass/fail system. They should start a campaign to rally support and make their small STEP team seem like an organization of 600 students instead of only six. They should start a dialogue between students and administrators.

The jobs were described and given a deadline for completion. Each job was assigned to a particular group member.

DIVIDE AND CONQUER

Once your team lists objectives and thoroughly discusses each one, it's time to divide the work. At the University of Missouri, one STEP member was an art student. She volunteered to head the publicity campaign. Another student felt comfortable speaking, so he volunteered to talk with administrators. Each member took on tasks according to his or her strengths.

Be honest about your abilities: Don't claim to possess strengths you don't have.

As your team divides labor, volunteer for things you feel more confident about. Offer to do extra legwork to help other members whose schedules

✍ EXERCISE

Pretend you're on a committee of students who want to do away with all grades at your high school. What's your plan? List three goals and three to five objectives that will help you reach each goal.

may be more hectic. However, be honest about your abilities: Don't claim to possess strengths you don't have.

COUNT ON TROUBLE

The time to anticipate problems is before you start. Brainstorm disasters. Ask what could possibly go wrong. Devise counterplans and contingencies. You have to be ready to react to the unforeseen.

As each of you heads out in different directions, plan to meet regularly as a team to mark your progress. Assume that other team members are giving their best, even if it doesn't look that way. If someone is having difficulties or working slower that the rest of the group, offer to help rather than criticize that person's performance.

The STEP team thought they might run into opposition from the faculty. To head that off, they conducted a survey of faculty opinions on pass/fail

Assume that other team members are giving their best, even if it doesn't look that way.

programs and shared the results. They held a faculty forum to help change opinions. However, what they hadn't anticipated was opposition from students. A large group of students opposed pass/fail classes. To address these students, the STEP team had to make on-the-spot changes in their campaign. No team can anticipate all obstacles. But if you anticipate some of the potential problems, you will be ready to deal with any additional surprises. STEP was eventually successful in getting pass/fail courses introduced to its university, but it took a lot of hard work, careful planning, and teamwork to meet their goals. Keep the following tips in mind the next time you work as a member of a team toward a goal.

TEAM CONSENSUS AND NEGOTIATIONS

It's not easy convincing one person to go along with your plan. So how can you get your whole team to agree with you? You don't. You work with your team toward a consensus, an agreement all of you can live with. You negotiate.

Negotiation isn't something new for you. You do it every day. Does this scenario sound familiar?

"Come home right after school," your Mom says, as you dash out the door one morning.

"But I promised to meet Ken after school. Is 6:00 okay?" you plead.

"Supper's at 5:30. How about home at 4:30?"

"Would 5:00 work?"

SECRETS TO TEAM GOAL SETTING

- Each member must take personal responsibility for goals.

- Every member needs to voice an opinion.

- Each opinion (no matter how far out) should be weighed and considered carefully.

- Team members need to volunteer to handle tasks that suit their abilities and strengths.

- Members must keep their individual commitments.

- Team members should help each other achieve objectives.

- The team shares the victory (or in some cases, the blame).

"All right, 5:00, but don't be late."

"Thanks, Mom."

And your negotiation is successful. Consider another example: At school on Wednesday, you ask your speech teacher if you can give your presentation last, which would be on Monday. She had you scheduled for today, but lets you off the hook until Friday. You agree. That night, you ask your dad for the car. Negotiations start all over again.

Two team members discuss strategy during a meeting. (C. Devan/zefa, Corbis)

As you can see, you negotiate all day. You don't solve problems by arguing to get your way. Instead, you work with others toward a solution both sides can live with.

Teamwork requires constant negotiation. As your team makes goals and sets strategies to achieve those goals, you'll have to come together and build a consensus. The result should be something each member can support—not one strong person's idea and not a majority's opinion. Your team needs a consensus.

Teamwork requires constant negotiation.

BOOKS ABOUT NEGOTIATING

Babcock, Linda, and Sara Laschever. *Women Don't Ask: The High Cost of Avoiding Negotiation—and Positive Strategies for Change.* New York: Bantam, 2007.

Dawson, Roger. *Secrets of Power Negotiating.* 2d ed. Franklin Lakes, N.J.: Career Press, 2000.

Fisher, Roger, and Alan Sharp. *Getting It Done: How to Lead When You're Not in Charge.* New York: Collins Business, 1999.

Harvard Business Essentials Guide to Negotiation. Cambridge, Mass.: Harvard Business School Press, 2003.

Malhotra, Deepak, and Max Bazerman. *Negotiation Genius: How to Overcome Obstacles and Achieve Brilliant Results at the Bargaining Table and Beyond.* New York: Bantam, 2008.

Raiffa, Howard, John Richardson, and David Metcalfe. *Negotiation Analysis: The Science and Art of Collaborative Decision Making.* Cambridge, Mass.: Belknap Press, 2007.

Shell, G. Richard. *Bargaining for Advantage: Negotiation Strategies for Reasonable People.* 2d ed. New York: Penguin Books, 2006.

Volkema, Roger J. *The Negotiation Toolkit: How to Get Exactly What You Want in Any Business or Personal Situation.* New York: AMACOM Books, 1999.

✍ EXERCISE

Imagine you are trying to bring two friends to a consensus. They disagree on where you should eat. One wants Dairy Queen, and the other wants Taco Bell. How could you solve this dilemma?

FOUR STAGES OF TEAM DEVELOPMENT

Most work teams go through a transition on their way to becoming effective. The process usually moves through four stages: on guard, duel, healing, and victory.

The On-Guard Stage

In the first stage, team members are "on guard." They have just formed a new team. Politeness reigns. No one wants to step on anybody's toes or look stupid. There's little overt friction or conflict, but there's not much creativity either. Since irritations aren't expressed openly, resentment can build up. The on-guard phase may look like a success because team members are agreeing so easily, but don't be fooled. If your team never progresses beyond this polite beginning, you'll never function as a strong team.

BARRIERS TO TEAM NEGOTIATIONS

• Failure to listen

• Fear of losing face

• Pride

• Fear of looking foolish

• Failure to take personal responsibility for outcome

What can you do to help move out of the on-guard stage? Don't sacrifice politeness, but feel free to ask sincere questions. Say, "I don't understand how that would work." Be brave enough to make other suggestions. Ask, "What do you think about . . . ?"

Defer to experience, but know that one of your offbeat ideas you're wary to share might be just what your team needs.

The Duel Stage

The second stage of team development can turn into a duel. Most people can hold back resentment only so long; something has to give. In the duel stage, tempers flare. The team divides over an issue, forming warring factions, each side resolving never to give an inch. Discussions move from controlled,

This team is stuck in the duel stage in which petty resentments create cliques that threaten team unity. Team members can get past the duel stage by finding common ground, compromising, and respecting the ideas and opinions of others. (ColorBlind Images, Corbis)

short talks to shouting matches. Needless to say, the team gets nowhere.

This duel stage is where many teams dissolve and quit trying. They may think that they can work more effectively on their own. Why bother working with a group of contrary people? They feel it's not worth the effort.

However, if people can understand the process of coming together as a team, they can move through the dueling stage and discover the true benefits of teamwork. How can you help your team move to the next stage? First, find positive points in the opinions held by opposing team members. Then try to come up with alternatives. When arguments divide your team, no one faction will win support. A new course of action has to be decided upon. If the team can agree on an alternative plan, you'll be on your way to the next stage.

When arguments divide your team, no one faction will win support.

The Healing Stage
In the healing stage, team members settle down and ease into a routine of compromise. Ideas are exchanged. People start to listen to each other and learn from each other, rather than trying to win oth-

"TIMES" IN TEAM NEGOTIATIONS

Most negotiations have each of the following moments:

- A time to listen—even to ideas you don't like
- A time to speak—bite your tongue when it's not
- A time to mediate—focus and clear up misunderstandings
- A time to learn—see the other side
- A time to compromise—find an alternative
- A time to accept—and change
- A time to support—and grow

ers over. Teams may devise their own ways of getting to a compromise, for example, by setting a 10-minute limit on discussions. During this stage, the team begins to see that the group working together can be more effective than the same individuals working independently. In the healing stage, teams begin to develop a sense of timing.

The Victory Stage

If the team hangs in there, healing will come—healing that leads to victory. This is the stage when teamwork pays off. A mutual respect among members frees everyone to take risks. All ideas are expressed, so the team can benefit from the best elements of each person's suggestion. From here, the best plan develops with contributions from everyone.

The following are comments from members of a high school academic team with a goal to fundraise for new equipment:

- "When we were finished [raising money], I couldn't even tell you who had done what. We had all accomplished what we wanted, and that was what mattered."

- "Everybody worked as hard as they could. So even though some of us may have looked like we did more, our team knew the credit belonged to everybody."

- "I didn't like the project we decided on, selling mums at homecoming. But I respected my teammates and threw myself

A mutual respect among members frees everyone to take risks.

✍ EXERCISE

Think about all the teams you've participated in, from class-project teams, to chess teams, to soccer teams. Write down the four stages of team development. Next to each one, jot down a memory from your team experiences that fits each stage. Describe how you progressed or failed to move on to the next stage of development.

into supporting the idea just as if I'd come up with it myself. I still don't think it was the best plan, but that didn't matter once we'd settled on it."

The students reached the highest teamwork phase, the victory stage, and discovered that their compromising and teamwork paid off.

✔ TRUE OR FALSE: ANSWERS

Do You Know How to Set Goals and Negotiate?

1. Team goals should be precise and match the overall goals of my company.

True. It is important to develop concise goals that match your company's mission statement or project objective.

2. You can still meet goals as a team even if half the members aren't contributing.

False. Every member of a team must contribute to ensure success. Sure, some goals may be met when only a few workers pitch in, but no team has ever been successful at half-speed.

3. Teamwork requires constant negotiation.

True. Good teams feature members who are willing to participate in give-and-take in order to meet project goals and objectives.

IN SUMMARY . . .

- Step one in setting team goals is to define the main goal. Behind this goal are your company's goals. Make sure that the goals of your team match up with your company's goals and mission statement.

- Good goals are specific and measurable.

- Strong teams consist of members who ALL get a chance to contribute toward goals.

- Working toward a goal should involve the following steps: breaking the goal into objectives; dividing the labor; anticipating and planning for problems, disasters, and objections; reaching team consensus through negotiation; and implementing the plan.

- There are four stages of team development: the on-guard stage, the duel stage, the healing stage, and the victory stage.

7

AVOIDING
TEAM-KILLING
BEHAVIORS

You'll be surprised by the influence you can have on your team, even as a rookie. You can encourage your team and lead them to success, or you can tear down unity with proven team killers. It's up to you.

Here are some of the major team-killing behaviors found in the workplace. If you can avoid these behaviors, you will be a good influence on your team—making your team more cohesive and successful.

GOSSIP

Robyn works with a medical team in a hospital in the Northeast. "Gossip can hurt our team like no other disease. Hospitals are notorious grapevines of gossip; it hurts our relationships. You get so you're afraid to say anything," Robyn says.

✔ TRUE OR FALSE?

Are You a Team Killer?

1. All gossip is bad.

2. My life should be an open book at work.

3. It is important to always be on time to work, be positive, and demonstrate ethical behavior.

Test yourself as you read through this chapter. The answers appear on page 148.

Gossip is destructive, and there's no room for it on a team.

One solution to curb team gossip is to keep your complaints and criticisms on a "need-to-know" basis. Does the person you're talking to need to know this information about a third party? Is that juicy tidbit about your boss something your team needs to hear? If the information is something you think your team or supervisor should know, be sure of your facts. Don't pass along someone else's gossip.

Next, to avoid being the subject of gossip, keep your personal life to yourself. Separate your professional life from your personal life. Don't give gossiping coworkers ammunition with stories of your love life or failures. Don't talk about how broke, bored, or unhappy you are—which hopefully you are not!

The most effective solution to putting a stop to team gossip is to pass along *good gossip*. Make a point

THE LEADING TEAM KILLERS

- Gossip
- Jealousy
- Prejudice
- Critical spirit
- Selfishness
- Laziness
- Stubbornness
- Negativism
- Blame
- Deceit

to share positive information with team members. If you're with your coworker Bill when he comments that Rhonda, another member of your team, is doing a great job with the Hansen account, tell Rhonda the next time you see her. If the boss wants you to write a report like Bill's because "Bill knows what he's doing," be sure to tell Bill the boss's positive remark.

Compliments delivered by a third party are the most valued of all because we know they're sincere. Rhonda wasn't even around when Bill paid her the

✍ EXERCISE

Most of us have been victims *and* perpetrators of gossip. Think about the last time you were a gossiper. Remember, this even includes passing along another person's gossip. Did the gossip change the way you felt about the person it was about? How could you have changed your comment to make it "good gossip?"

compliment, so she knows he wasn't flattering her or trying to be nice. If you pass along good gossip, you'll exert a powerful influence. Good gossip can transform an office.

I will speak ill of no man and speak all the good I know of everybody.

—**Benjamin Franklin, American inventor and statesman**

Jealousy usually springs from individual insecurities.

JEALOUSY

Jealousy usually springs from individual insecurities. This can cause unhealthy competition to develop among team members. One person may withhold helpful information from another. Another worker might not offer to help with tasks that are not in his or her job description. The result is a team that operates like competitors.

What can you do? First, don't be pulled into jealous competition with your teammates. Offer to help them succeed. Don't compare yourself with your teammates. Instead, know that you're doing your best. Suggest to your team that you turn the competition outward. Compete with your business competitors, not your coworkers.

When we have a brilliant idea, instead of making others think it is ours, why not let them cook and stir the idea themselves. They will then regard it as their own.

—William Winter, writer

PREJUDICE

Your team won't stand a chance if you tolerate prejudice in any form. Some business teams have unofficial "old boys' clubs"—no women allowed. Other teams divide along racial or cultural lines.

As a worker just starting out, your best chance to influence your team is in your personal relationships with teammates. Try to develop solid relationships with everyone on your team. Be careful of subtle prejudices, such as choosing your friends by personality or by how much they're like you.

Try to develop solid relationships with everyone on your team.

Beware of silent complicity. Don't be afraid to speak up when you see prejudiced behavior. In addition, never laugh at cruel jokes or racial comments.

Beliefs and stereotypes are so deeply ingrained and yet they are learned. They are not natural in our genes. We are not born with those stereotypes. We learn them. And many times, those stereotypes are taught at such an early age, when we are shaping our values and beliefs, that we do not recall them.

The media is one of the major shapers of ideology, beliefs, and values. Even if it seems innocent, like a television program, it is sending stereotypical messages. For many years, there was an absence of (different) races of people on television. In that absence there are messages: insignificance.

—Gladys Gossett Hankins, Ph.D.,
Cincinnati Enquirer

BEING CRITICAL

It doesn't take great creativity to notice faults in other people. If you are critical of your team, you can dampen enthusiasm and impede success. Don't be quick to point out flaws in the company or in the way your team conducts business. Don't waste your time criticizing other people.

It doesn't hurt you to believe the best of people. If your coworker Mary says she tried her hardest but couldn't get her part done in time, you might as well believe her and offer to help. Better to believe the best than assume the worst.

Better to believe the best than assume the worst.

Any fool can criticize, condemn, and complain—and most fools do.

—Dale Carnegie, writer and lecturer

Another way to fight team-killing criticism is to "catch people being good." Some people lie in wait, hoping to catch others making mistakes. Instead, be on the alert for good things people do. Catch them doing good work and praise them for it—directly and to others. For example, you could comment to a coworker, "Did you see the way John handled himself in that meeting? He knew just what to say." Or you could tell John, "I appreciated the way you handled the client meeting this morning." Praise loudly; criticize softly.

SELFISHNESS

From the moment you join a team, you need to shift gears. Your success now depends on how well your team performs, not on how good you look.

Selfishness may make you volunteer for the showy jobs or the tasks that don't require as much time or energy. Selfishness can keep you from sharing information that would help someone else.

The answer to selfishness is generosity. Look for ways to help your team. Remember, your own success depends on their success. Do more than your share.

LAZINESS

Laziness will kill a team. The old saying about a chain being only as strong as its weakest link applies to teamwork. If you don't do your part, the whole team fails. This isn't high school, where you might get an extension on an assignment or talk a teacher into letting you off the hook. You can't cram the night before a test or copy someone else's work. In the working world, you have to do just that, work. To top it off, much of your hard work will be done without praise, because now it is expected of you.

Failure is not our only punishment for laziness: There is also the success of others.

—Jules Renard, French author

Write down your commitments to your team, and keep those commitments.

Some teams form a contract of commitment, such as, *I agree to show up on time or early, I'll contribute to discussions,* etc. If your team has no such contract, make one for yourself. Write down your commitments to your team, and keep those commitments.

Laziness includes showing up late, leaving early, wasting time, procrastinating, and failing to do what you say you will. If you bring laziness to your team, you not only kill your team—you just may lose your job.

STUBBORNNESS

Part of good team spirit is the spirit of compromise. Be willing to learn from your team. Don't come to meetings with your mind made up, because stubbornness and inflexibility can kill your team. Your job isn't to win everyone over to your way of thinking. You need to move with your team toward a consensus, a solution you can all agree on.

Take on the role of mediator. In meetings, jot down what people say. When an agreement is reached, get it in writing. Then, when arguments erupt, you can refer to your notes and get your team back on track.

NEGATIVISM

Your team may come up with goals and plans you don't think will work. Still, don't bring negativism to your team. Don't be the one who always says, "That won't work." If you have doubts, ask questions. Ask, "What would happen if. . .?" Or, "Would it be better to. . . ?"

Bring solutions to your team rather than problems.

NEGATIVE STYLES

Internal Negativity: Mental Attitudes

- The Workaholic

- The Controller

- The Know-it-All

External Negativity: Behavior and Actions

- The Back-Stabber

- The Rabble-Rouser

- The Martyr

Verbal Negativity: Words

- The Gossip

- The Cynic

- The Apathetic

Source: *Overcoming Negativity in the Workplace,* Change Dynamics (a business training consulting firm)

Focus on the positives. No matter how wild an idea, you can probably find something positive about it. Even if you can't, you still don't have to dismiss it completely.

Bring solutions to your team rather than problems. If you're having difficulty with your part of the project, don't come to your team meeting complaining and empty-handed. Show up with an alternative plan or at least a couple of ideas. Difficulties can be viewed as disasters or challenges. It's all in how you look at it.

BLAME

When something doesn't work out right with your team project, resist the urge to blame someone. Don't ask, "Who did this?" Instead, ask, "Why did this happen?" It doesn't matter whose fault it is. If you can help discover why the problem occurred, you can help your team avoid it next time.

DECEIT

Deceit will kill your team and your relationships. Always be honest with your teammates. Of course, you don't have to tell them everything. However, what you do tell them should be true.

Don't pretend to understand something you don't. Don't try to bluff your way through a project. Instead, ask questions and learn.

ADOPT A NEW VIEW

Most of the team killers manifest themselves when workers put their own needs ahead of their team. But becoming a part of a team means putting team success ahead of your own. Centuries ago, a man named

Ptolemy came up with a system to explain the world. He decided our planet was the center of the universe and that the moon, sun, planets and stars revolved around us. His ideas were accepted as truth for thousands of years until a man named Copernicus proved him wrong. Copernicus discovered that that the earth was not the center of the universe but instead traveled around the sun with the other planets.

V-I-C-T-O-R-Y!

Join the ranks of professionals who have found personal victory through teamwork:

Small groups are, quite simply, the basic organizational building blocks of excellent companies.
        —Thomas J. Peters and Robert H. Waterman, Jr.,
                *In Search of Excellence: Lessons from
                        America's Best-Run Companies*

We look for people who know how to work on a team. When you get people who know how to help and be helped, who understand that if the company folds, they fold too—then your company is going to succeed.
                —Al Hershberger, national sales manager,
                        Custer Products Incorporated

The founder of Hewlett-Packard explains his company's victory: "There is a feeling that everyone is part of a

Many of us grow up as the center of our own universe. As a child, your mottos might have been "look out for number one," "I've got to be my own person," and "I want to do it my way." Well, in the working world, you aren't the center anymore; you're part of a team. Welcome to the (working) universe.

team, and that team is H. P. It exists because people have seen that it works, and they believe that this feeling makes H. P. what it is."

—Bill Hewitt in Peters and Waterman's
In Search of Excellence

Everything here at Disneyland and the Studio is a team effort. I credit the success of my films to the teamwork in my organization.

—Walt Disney in *Walt Disney: Famous Quotes*

There is a special relationship between Delta and its personnel that is rarely found in any firm, generating a team spirit that is evident in the individual's cooperative attitude toward others, cheerful outlook toward life and pride in a job well done.

—Delta representative
in Peters and Waterman's
In Search of Excellence

✔ TRUE OR FALSE: ANSWERS

Are You a Team Killer?

1. All gossip is bad.

False. Negative gossip is always bad. But there is another type of gossip that's acceptable in the workplace and may help fuel team success. Good gossip is positive information or comments about an individual that is passed along to that person by a third party (for example, "He said you did a great job on the project." or "She said you're really catching on quickly to the new software program."). This type of gossip builds people up and encourages them, rather than tears them down.

2. My life should be an open book at work.

False. Your team does not need to know about your love life, financial problems, or other personal concerns. Talking about your personal life may reflect negatively on you and cause team members to lose respect for you.

3. It is important to always be on time to work, be positive, and demonstrate ethical behavior.

True. Be a model employee and team member by avoiding negative behaviors in the workplace. You will gain your colleagues' respect and increase your chances of promotion and overall success in the workplace.

IN SUMMARY . . .

- The ability of a team can be killed by the following: gossip, jealousy, prejudice, being critical, selfishness, laziness, stubbornness, negativism, blame, and deceit.

- Instead of avoiding all gossip, try passing along good gossip about coworkers who deserve recognition for their hard work.

- Don't compete with your own team members; compete with your outside business competitors.

- Prejudice of any kind should never be tolerated in the workplace.

- Instead of being critical of others, believe in them.

- The answer to selfishness is generosity.

- Make verbal or written commitments to your team to avoid laziness.

- Stay flexible when working with others.

- View work difficulties as challenges instead of disasters.

- Instead of worrying about who created a problem, concentrate on how and why it happened.

- Be true to your team, in your actions and your words.

WEB SITES

Body Language

Answers.com: Body Language
  http://www.answers.com/topic/body-language

Gestures: Body Language and Nonverbal
  Communication
  http://www.csupomona.edu/~tassi/gestures.
  htm#gestures

Conflict Resolution

Association for Conflict Resolution
  http://www.acrnet.org

Center for Conflict Resolution
  http://www.ccrchicago.org

Conflict Information Consortium
  http://conflict.colorado.edu

Institute for Conflict Analysis and Resolution
  http://icar.gmu.edu

Diversity

Diversity Inc.
   http://www.diversityinc.com

Workplace Diversity
   http://www.workplacediversity.com

Dress, Business

About.com: Business Casual Dress Code
   http://humanresources.about.com/od/
   glossaryd/g/dress_code.htm

Business Casual Attire
   http://www.career.vt.edu/JOBSEARC/BusCasual.htm

How to Dress Business Casual—Men
   http://www.ehow.com/how_41_dress-business-
   casual.html

How to Dress Business Casual—Women
   http://www.ehow.com/how_49_dress-business-
   casual.html

General

Manual for Working in Teams
   http://www.analytictech.com/mb021/teamhint.
   htm

Surviving the Group Project: A Note on Working in
   Teams
   http://web.cba.neu.edu/~ewertheim/teams/
   ovrvw2.htm#Introduction

Team Building
   http://www.meetingwizard.org/meetings/team-building.cfm

13 Ways to Encourage Teamwork
   http://www.askmen.com/money/successful_100/115_success.html

Goal Setting

About Goal Setting: The 20-Minute Tutorial
   http://www.about-goal-setting.com

eHow: How to Set Goals
   www.ehow.com/how_2048963_set-goals.html

Goal Setting for Everyone
   http://www.mygoals.com

Goal Setting: Powerful Written Goals in 7 Easy
   Steps
   http://www.topachievement.com/goalsetting.html

Personal Goal Setting: Planning to Live Life Your
   Own Way
   http://www.mindtools.com/page6.html

Setting Goals
   http://www.xsitepro.com/Setting-Goals.pdf

Mentors

MENTOR/National Mentoring Partnership
   http://www.mentoring.org

MentorNet: The E-Mentoring Network for Diversity in Engineering and Science
http://www.mentornet.net

Professional Coaches and Mentors Association
http://www.pcmaonline.com

Women's Rights

Women's Rights at Work
http://www.citizenactionny.org

Workplace Rights

Equal Employment Opportunity Commission
http://www.eeoc.gov

Equality and Human Rights Commission
http://www.equalityhumanrights.com

Harassment Hotline Inc.
http://www.end-harassment.com

Women's Rights at Work
http://www.citizenactionny.org

WorkRelationships Inc.
http://www.workrelationships.com

GLOSSARY

adapting behavior adjusting and modifying the way one acts in order to fit in

body language the gestures, movements, and mannerisms a person uses to intentionally or unintentionally communicate moods and opinions to others

choleric one of the four temperaments; confident, goal oriented, and capable

company culture the customs, ways and procedures of a company and its way of doing business

compromise to settle differences of opinion by mutual agreement and concession

confrontation a meeting of two or more parties with clashing interests or ideas

consensus general agreement of opinion

diversity the condition of being diverse; in a work setting, this term is most often applied to groups of people who share basic human characteristics, but who have noticeable differences including gender, country of origin, culture, ethnic background, religion, and level of education

duel stage the second stage in team development; initial politeness gives way to anger and factions, with each side resolving never to give an inch

empowerment to promote self-actualization; in a work setting, to give employees power or authority to make decisions that were at one time only made by managers

fair play impartial treatment

goal the desired end toward which work is directed

goal oriented motivated by the achievement of goals and objectives

good gossip information of a positive nature passed along to others about another person; good gossip builds the reputation of an individual and encourages successful teamwork

healing stage the third stage of team development; team members settle down and ease into a routine of compromise, exchanging ideas, and learning from each other

interpersonal skills the knowledge and ability to get along well with people; tools to help build personal relationships

learning style an individual's preferred method for acquiring information

mediator one who intervenes between two or more disagreeing individuals or groups to promote reconciliation and compromise

melancholy one of the four temperaments; artistic, organized, analytical, and sensitive

mentor an unofficial teacher, coach, or adviser

mission statement a brief description of a company or other organization's purpose and goals of existence multicultural reflecting many cultures

negotiation the process of coming to mutual agreement between two parties

objective a goal in a project

on-guard stage the first stage in team development; team members remain polite and cautious, reluctant to voice dissenting opinions

people oriented motivated by relationships and the desire for everyone to get along and do well

people smart the ability to figure out what others need and want and to handle personal relationships successfully

phlegmatic one of the four temperaments; generally easygoing, well balanced, and steady

priorities tasks, people, or events that are given attention before other alternatives

sanguine one of the four temperaments; outgoing, life of the party, popular

sexual harassment offensive and uninvited verbal or physical conduct directed toward a person because of his or her sex

teamwork the process of a group of people pooling their resources and skills to work together and achieve a common goal

temperament one's nature or customary frame of mind and natural disposition

unwritten rules required behavior that is expected but not stated in any manual, meeting, etc.

victory stage the fourth and final stage of team development; the group has achieved unity and accomplishes more than they would as individuals

BIBLIOGRAPHY

Andersen, Peter. *The Complete Idiot's Guide to Body Language*. New York: Alpha, 2004.

Avery, Christopher M., Meri Aaron Walker, and Erin O'Toole. *Teamwork Is an Individual Skill: Getting Your Work Done When Sharing Responsibility*. San Francisco: Berrett-Koehler Publishers, 2001.

Babcock, Linda, and Sara Laschever. *Women Don't Ask: The High Cost of Avoiding Negotiation—and Positive Strategies for Change*. New York: Bantam, 2007.

Boland, Mary. *Sexual Harassment in the Workplace*. Naperville, Ill.: Sphinx Publishing, 2005.

Cox, Taylor, Jr. *Creating the Multicultural Organization: A Strategy for Capturing the Power of Diversity*. San Francisco: Jossey-Bass, 2001.

CultureGrams 2009 World Edition. Ann Arbor, Mich.: Proquest LLC, 2008.

Dawson, Roger. *Secrets of Power Negotiating*. 2d ed. Franklin Lakes, N.J.: Career Press, 2000.

Dresser, Norine. *Multicultural Manners: Essential Rules of Etiquette for the 21st Century.* Rev. ed. Hoboken, N.J.: Wiley, 2005.

Fisher, Roger, and Alan Sharp. *Getting It Done: How to Lead When You're Not in Charge.* New York: Collins Business, 1999.

Gregory, Raymond F. *Unwelcome and Unlawful: Sexual Harassment in the American Workplace.* Ithaca, N.Y.: Cornell University Press, 2004.

Harvard Business Essentials Guide to Negotiation. Cambridge, Mass.: Harvard Business School Press, 2003.

Henderson, Veronique, and Pat Henshaw. *Image Matters for Men: How to Dress for Success!* London, U.K.: Hamlyn, 2007.

Howard, Linda Gordon. *The Sexual Harassment Handbook.* Franklin Lakes, N.J.: Career Press, 2007.

Kaip, Sarah. *The Woman's Workplace Survival Guide.* Medford, Oreg.: Advantage Source, 2005.

Konrad, Alison M., Pushkala Prasad, and Judith K. Pringle, eds. *Handbook of Workplace Diversity.* Thousand Oaks, Calif.: Sage Publications, 2006.

Kuhnke, Elizabeth. *Body Language For Dummies.* Hoboken, N.J.: For Dummies, 2007.

Lenius, Oscar. *A Well-Dressed Gentleman's Pocket Guide.* London, U.K.: Prion, 2006.

Lerner, Dick. *Dress Like the Big Fish: How to Achieve the Image You Want and the Success You Deserve.* Omaha, Neb.: Bel Air Fashions Press, 2008

Levy, Anne C., and Michele A. Paludi. *Workplace Sexual Harassment.* 2d ed. Upper Saddle River, N.J.: Prentice Hall, 2001.

Malhotra, Deepak, and Max Bazerman. *Negotiation Genius: How to Overcome Obstacles and Achieve Brilliant Results at the Bargaining Table and Beyond.* New York: Bantam, 2008.

Maxwell, John C. *The 17 Essential Qualities of a Team Player: Becoming the Kind of Person Every Team Wants.* Nashville, Tenn.: Thomas Nelson, 2002.

Maxwell, John C. *The 17 Indisputable Laws of Teamwork Workbook: Embrace Them and Empower Your Team.* Nashville, Tenn.: Thomas Nelson, 2003.

Miller, Patrick W. *Body Language on the Job.* Munster, Ind.: Patrick W. Miller & Associates, 2006.

Mogil, Marc. *I Know What You're Really Thinking: Reading Body Language Like a Trial Lawyer.* Bloomington, Ind.: 1st Books Library, 2003.

Mor Barak, Michalle E. *Managing Diversity: Toward a Globally Inclusive Workplace.* Thousand Oaks, Calif.: Sage Publications, 2005.

Parker, Glenn M. *Team Players and Teamwork: New Strategies for Developing Successful Collaboration.* 2d ed. San Francisco: Jossey-Bass, 2008.

Peragine, John N. *365 Low or No Cost Workplace Teambuilding Activities: Games and Exercises Designed to Build Trust & Encourage Teamwork Among Employees.* Ocala, Fla.: Atlantic Publishing Company, 2008.

Peres, Daniel. *Details Men's Style Manual: The Ultimate Guide for Making Your Clothes Work for You.* New York: Gotham, 2007.

Peters, Thomas J., and Robert H. Waterman. *In Search of Excellence: Lessons from America's Best-Run Companies.* New York: Collins Business, 2004.

Raiffa, Howard, John Richardson, and David Metcalfe. *Negotiation Analysis: The Science and Art of Collaborative Decision Making.* Cambridge, Mass.: Belknap Press, 2007.

Reiman, Tonya. *The Power of Body Language.* New York: Pocket, 2007.

Samovar, Larry A., Richard E. Porter, and Edwin R. McDaniel. *Intercultural Communication: A Reader.* 12th ed. Florence, Ky.: Wadsworth Publishing, 2008.

Shell, G. Richard. *Bargaining for Advantage: Negotiation Strategies for Reasonable People.* 2d ed. New York: Penguin Books, 2006.

Stowell, Steven J., and Stephanie S. Mead. *The Team Approach: With Teamwork Anything Is Possible.* Sandy, Utah: CMOE Press, 2007.

Thiederman, Sondra. *Making Diversity Work: 7 Steps for Defeating Bias in the Workplace.* Rev. ed. New York: Kaplan Publishing, 2008.

Tieger, Paul D., and Barbara Barron. *Do What You Are: Discover the Perfect Career for You Through the Secrets of Personality Type.* Rev. ed. New York: Little, Brown and Company, 2007.

Volkema, Roger J. *The Negotiation Toolkit: How to Get Exactly What You Want in Any Business or Personal Situation.* New York: AMACOM Books, 1999.

Weingarten, Rachel C. *Career and Corporate Cool.* Hoboken, N.J.: Wiley, 2007.

Index